MATHS MASTERY

A PARENT'S GUIDE TO HELPING YOUR CHILD
SCORE 100/100 IN MATHS

AMRITA AGARWAL

INDIA • SINGAPORE • MALAYSIA

Copyright © Amrita Agarwal 2024
All Rights Reserved.

ISBN 979-8-89066-795-3

About the Author

Amrita Agarwal, an Academic Strategist, brings a wealth of experience when training students to achieve perfect scores in maths. Amrita's extensive background in both maths and technology has equipped her with unique skills that help cultivate in her students a strong foundation and love for learning maths. With her experience, she has refined her techniques and approaches to help students reach their full potential, fostering lasting relationships with students as well as parents.

Amrita believes in the universal language of maths, leveraging her diverse educational background to integrate various teaching methods. With a *Master's in Business Administration* from *India*, a *Master's in Computer Science* from the *University of Southern California, USA*, and experience from a *Japanese Education Institute*, her approach is tailored to meet every student's individual needs. Collaborating closely with each student, Amrita crafts personalised learning plans to instil a lifelong love for maths and learning.

With her dedication and expertise, Amrita has helped numerous students excel academically across various countries and educational systems. She emphasises real-life skills like time management, self-study, and independent learning, facilitated by her *S-9 Framework*. Amrita also provides practical strategies for parents to support their child's mathematical excellence. Her teachings focus on fundamental principles and their real-world applications, inspiring both students and parents to stay motivated and engaged.

Amrita can be contacted through the following channels:

Email: team@amritaagarwal.com

Website: www.amritaagarwal.com

LinkedIn: https://www.linkedin.com/in/amrita-agarwal-89a32515

Instagram: https://www.instagram.com/amrita.agarwal87/

Facebook: https://www.facebook.com/amrita.agarwal.35

This book is dedicated to all the teachers and mentors who have played a vital role in shaping my journey. Some have taught and guided me directly, while others have impacted me through their books and experiences. Your guidance has been invaluable, and I am forever grateful.

Contents

Section 3 Fears and Stress

Section 4 Mastering Exams   95

Section 5 Mindfulness and Happiness

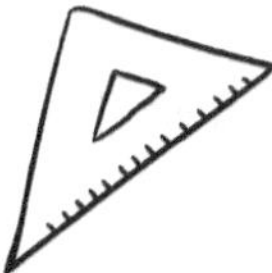

Introduction

Welcome to *"Maths Mastery: A Parent's Guide to Ensuring Your Child Achieves 100/100 in Maths"*. This book isn't about quick fixes or overnight transformations. Instead, it's a journey towards fostering a deep and lasting understanding of mathematics in your child – a skill that transcends mere exam scores and becomes a foundation for lifelong success.

Mathematics isn't just a subject; it's the language of the universe that we are a part of. I firmly believe that nurturing a love for maths in your child goes beyond academic achievements; it empowers him/her to navigate the world with confidence and clarity.

My passion for maths led me to become a Maths Educator, wherein I've dedicated myself to helping parents like you unlock their children's full mathematical potential. Through my experiences, I've realised that mastering maths is akin to climbing a ladder—one step at a time—each step building upon the last.

I understand the concerns and aspirations regarding your children's education. The frustration of seeing them struggle despite their potential is something many parents face. But fear not; this book is crafted precisely for parents like you who seek to support their children's mathematical journey.

Whether you're daunted by maths or feel unqualified to teach it, this book will equip you with the tools and confidence to guide your child through their mathematical endeavours. Drawing from my experiences and success stories, I present the transformative *"S-9 Framework of Maths Mastery"*.

This framework isn't just about achieving perfect scores; it's about fostering a growth mindset, instilling motivation, and creating a supportive learning environment at home. From practical guidance to effective problem-solving strategies, this book is your roadmap to mathematical excellence for your child.

But it doesn't stop there. Educators and tutors will also find invaluable insights within these pages to enhance their teaching practises and support their students' academic journey.

Let's embark on this journey of transforming your child's maths experience together. With "Maths Mastery" as your trusted companion, it will pave the way for your child's mathematical success – one step at a time.

I would love to hear from you! Share your thoughts, feedback, or the stories that you've experienced through the book. Your stories will inspire me and help me continue to make a difference.

If someone has recommended or gifted this book to you, please extend my heartfelt gratitude to them.

I've created a Math Mastery Resource bundle for you, which includes the templates, timetables, posters, and all other resources mentioned in the book. You can print them out and get started. Additionally, the resource bundle contains a Canva template and a tutorial to create a special poster for your child.

To receive your Resource Bundle, click this link: https://amritaagarwal.com/mmr/

Be rest assured, that if you encounter any difficulties while downloading, please don't hesitate to reach out to our team at team@amritaagarwal.com.

SECTION 1

WHY PARENTS STRUGGLE
AND FEEL
MATHS EXCELLENCE IS TOUGH FOR
THEIR CHILD

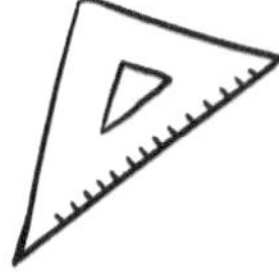

Chapter 1.1

Common Mistakes That Parents Make

Mathematics is a subject that requires attention to detail, patience, and consistent practise. Achieving a perfect score of 100/100 in maths can be challenging for both students and parents. However, many students and parents unknowingly make common mistakes that hinder their achievement. In this chapter, we will explore these mistakes and discuss overcoming them, which will help you fulfil your desire to see your child love maths and even score well in it.

1. Neglecting Early Maths Practise:

The most common mistake parents often make is not introducing daily maths practise to their children early on, thinking maths skills can wait until later. However, this leads to significant struggles as the child grows older.

Initially, all children are naturally inclined towards maths. However, as time passes and the gap between school learning and home practise widens, they begin to face difficulties. Unfortunately, by the time parents realise this, there is no time to bridge the gap effectively.

Example: Imagine a parent who wants their child to love maths. Instead of waiting for signs of struggle, they take proactive steps. The parent sets aside time for maths practise daily, seamlessly integrating it into their child's routine. They create engaging activities that make maths a natural part of their daily life, ensuring there are no missed learning opportunities.

Consistently incorporating maths into their routine exposes children to new concepts and skills, preventing gaps and building a solid maths foundation from an early age.

2. Lack of Belief in Your Child's Ability:

Another common mistake parents make is the lack of belief in a child's ability. Believing in your child's ability is essential. Provide them with the necessary support and encouragement to excel in maths. Building their confidence and belief in maths skills will positively impact their performance.

Example: Imagine your child is having trouble with long division. After numerous attempts and continued struggles, you may begin to worry, "*Maybe my child just isn't good at maths.*" You might inadvertently express this concern through your words or actions, influencing your child's perception of their abilities.

You might find yourself saying things like, "*Maths isn't everyone's cup of tea,*" or "*Maybe you inherited my maths struggles; I was never a numbers person either.*" You could suggest that they focus more on subjects where they're naturally more talented or even subtly encourage them to skim over the challenging division problems in their homework.

However, these actions, driven by your concerns, could unintentionally signal to your child that you lack confidence in their mathematical abilities.

But imagine a different scenario, one where you firmly believe in your child's potential to excel in maths despite the initial difficulties. Whenever your children struggle with any topic, you need to reassure them that **learning involves challenges and setbacks**. You should remind them of the past problems they've successfully overcome in other subjects, helping boost their confidence.

To support them in mastering long division, you might find step-by-step video tutorials or consult a professional to help them with their growth mindset. Your continual encouragement and faith in their abilities will motivate your children to persevere, which can significantly enhance their confidence and, eventually, their performance in maths.

3. Not Understanding 'Why':

Sometimes, you might know that your child is struggling with maths, but you might not have spent enough time figuring out *'why'*. It's essential to understand why they're finding it tough. The problem could be with the understanding of specific topics, or maybe they get nervous during tests.

Example: Once you know what's causing the problem, it becomes much easier to find the right kind of help needed. This could be finding more practise problems, helping them feel less nervous during tests, or getting a professional's help. So, if you take the time to understand the 'why', it's easier to find a way to make maths simpler for your child.

4. Not Showing That Maths Matters and Skipping Daily Practise:

Many parents understand the importance of maths and often communicate its significance to their children. However, children might need more than discussions alone to convey its real-life relevance effectively. Demonstrating maths in everyday applications can be a far more impactful way of instilling its value, especially for younger students. Show your child that maths isn't just numbers on a page. It's all around us! Explain how maths is practically used in fields like engineering, finance, and technology, or even in daily life, but in a fun way. Give examples of sports, racing cars, giant wheels, rockets, etc., whatever your child likes and relates with. This way, they'll see its real-life relevance and get excited about its possibilities.

Example: An activity can clarify the concept. Imagine you're at a food joint with your child. After ordering some snacks, the cashier tells you the total bill. Now, you can ask your child to help determine how much change you should receive from the cashier.

This moment is a great opportunity to show how useful maths can be in everyday situations. By helping your child understand how to calculate the change quickly, you show him/her how maths can be practical and helpful in real life, not just in school exams.

5. Insufficient Practise:

Another mistake is the lack of sufficient practise. In maths, it's not enough to just know about things. The real key to success is **mastering the concepts**. And the way to master them is through practise – lots and lots of practise. It's like learning to play a sport or an instrument – the more you practise, the better you get.

Why is practise so important? Well, in maths, we need to be fast and accurate. The more we practise, the quicker and more correct our answers become.

Example: Consider the addition problem 7 + 8. If your child has practised addition well, they'll know immediately that the answer is 15. But if they haven't, they might need to go through all the steps: start with 7 + 1, then 7 + 2, and so on, until they reach the answer. That takes a lot more time and effort. (*Imagine the nightmare they face later in life in competitive exams. It sends shivers down my spine*).

It's the same reason that we still remember nursery rhymes when we grow up. We sang them daily when we were little, so they're engraved in our minds. We mastered them through practise. So, just like we practised those rhymes, children should practise maths regularly. Over time, the things that once seemed hard will start to feel easy – and that's when you know you've mastered them.

6. Sole Reliance on School Practise:

Solely relying on the practise done in school is another common mistake that parents often make. While school practise is essential, more is needed to achieve maths success. It's crucial to supplement school practise with independent practise to reinforce learning and develop a deeper understanding of the concepts.

Example: In school, a child learns the basic multiplication tables. Initially, they might know the tables for 1 to 5. They practise them in school, get some homework, and then the class quickly moves to more advanced topics.

Then, when division starts in the school curriculum, a child with only minimum practise that was done in school might struggle to make the connections. They might need to count or use other time-consuming methods to solve the division problem because they haven't fully internalised the multiplication facts.

In contrast, children who practise multiplication regularly at home will find it easier to grasp the division. If they've mastered that 5*5 equals 25, then when asked what 25 divided by 5 is, they will quickly know the answer is 5.

This example clearly illustrates the importance of independent practise at home, reinforcing and deepening the understanding of the maths concepts learned in school. Combining school instruction with home practise provides the best platform for a child to master maths.

7. Total Dependence on Tutors:

Making students fully dependent on tutors is a mistake that can hinder your child's ability to think independently and develop problem-solving skills. While tutors can provide valuable guidance, you should encourage your child to tackle maths problems alone and think critically to solve them.

Example: Let's say your child has a hard time dividing numbers. A tutor could show them how to do every single step of the division problem. That would help your child get the answer right away.

However, a better way would be to let your child try the division problem independently, referring to a solved division problem. It is okay even if they make mistakes. The tutor can then help fix those mistakes and show your child where they went wrong and how to do it correctly. This way, you can gain valuable insights into the observation and understanding skills of the child. *(Next time you hire a tutor, look for educators who employ this method and observe closely).*

So, it's good for your child to try things first, with the tutor there to help when they get stuck or make mistakes. By testing and failing at first and then learning from the mistakes, your children would get better at dividing numbers all by themselves. This way, your child learns to do things independently and gets better, which would also help them think more and solve problems on their own instead of always relying on the tutor.

8. Lack of Strong Fundamentals:

Another common mistake is the need to build strong fundamentals. As we understand, maths follows a sequential structure, wherein concepts and skills are developed based on one another. Each new topic or skill relies on a solid understanding of those that came before. Children need a solid understanding of the foundational concepts to grasp more advanced topics. Hence, parents should ensure children have a strong maths foundation. Parents can help children focus on fundamental concepts before moving on to more complex ones.

Example: A child struggles to solve a maths problem like:

2/5 * (1/3 - 1/2) + 5

It might seem that the child is having trouble because they're not paying enough attention or are finding it too hard. However, the real issue might be that they don't fully understand some basic maths rules.

For example, to solve this problem, the child needs to know:

- Multiplication tables and division.

- They must also know how to add, subtract, multiply, and divide **fractions**. They also need to understand the order in which these operations need to be performed – that's something called the **BODMAS** rule.

If the child hasn't learned these basics well, they will find the problem hard even if they try their best. It's like trying to read a book when you don't know the alphabet; no matter how hard you try, you won't understand what the book says until you learn your ABCs.

And this doesn't just apply to this one problem. The further you go in maths, the more you'll need to rely on these essential skills. That's why ensuring children have a strong foundation in these basics is crucial. It's like building a tower; if the base isn't solid, it can't stand tall.

9. Neglecting to Review Previously Learned Material:

Refraining from reviewing previously learned material is another mistake that can hinder progress. As mentioned earlier, maths concepts are built upon one another, and therefore, it's essential to regularly review and reinforce formerly known material to maintain a strong foundation.

Example: Suppose your child is learning to multiply fractions in maths class.

7/9 * 8/5

They understand the concept:

   a. Multiply the numerators (top numbers) for the new numerator, and

   b. Multiply the denominators (bottom numbers) together for the new denominator.

But when it comes to actually doing the multiplication, they need help. That could be because your child needs to remember their multiplication tables, which they learned a few years ago. The ability to quickly multiply numbers is critical when working with fractions, and if your child has to struggle to remember that 7 times 8 is 56, for example, then multiplying fractions will be much more complex.

So, even though your child is now working on more advanced topics like fractions, it's still important to regularly review and practise basic skills like multiplication. Spend time studying the multiplication tables each week, ensuring your child has them down pat. By keeping these basic skills sharp, your child will have a much easier time with more advanced maths topics like fractions.

10. Rushing Through Problems and Neglecting Details:

Rushing through problems and neglecting to pay attention to details is a standard error that leads to careless mistakes. If you can identify where the child is rushing, you can encourage them to take their time there and double-check the work to ensure accuracy.

Example: Imagine your child is trying to solve 23×14. Ideally, they would do this:

23

*14

-----

92 (23 multiplied by 4)

230 (23 multiplied by 10)

------

322 (adding).

However, in their haste, they might just multiply the units placed (3 and 4) and get 12, writing down 2 and carrying over 1. Then, when multiplying the tens place, they forget to add the carry-over 1. This will lead to mistakes in their final answer. By observing them solve it step-by-step, you can identify where they are going wrong and remind them of the correct process.

In maths, students must follow simple steps to get the correct answer. First, they should read the question satisfactorily to understand what it's asking. Then, they should solve the problem step by step, using what they've learned. After they think they have the answer, it's a good idea to look over their work to check for any mistakes. While teachers in school can teach and tutors can guide, it's mainly up to the parents or subject matter experts to truly observe and instil these habits. Making your child practise maths daily, following the right approach, will reinforce the proper techniques.

This trend of overlooking details often develops further into adulthood as well. That creates further more problems for not just them but everyone around them – at work, at home, and in life. Watch out for it, and free your child from it immediately.

11. Hesitation to Seek Professional Help:

Some parents and students hesitate to seek help from professionals when facing challenges in maths. Consulting professionals can provide targeted support and guidance that is tailored to your child's specific needs, helping them overcome difficulties and build confidence in maths.

Example: Imagine your child is struggling with algebra, particularly with solving equations. They've attempted to work it out independently, but dealing with variables and constants is too confusing. As a parent, you are trying to help, and even their maths teacher is spending extra time with them, but you're all struggling to understand precisely where the difficulty lies.

Professionals can make a difference as they are trained and experienced in dealing with various learning styles and difficulties. They often have a good knack for pinpointing where the misunderstanding or confusion lies.

They might provide easy strategies and techniques to simplify solving and explaining things in a way that is attuned to your child's specific needs. This way, your child could understand how to solve these difficult problems. Not only would this solve their immediate problem, but could also build their confidence in handling other problems in the future. So, even if it feels uncomfortable, reaching out to professionals can often provide the exact help your child needs when struggling with maths.

Common Mistakes Parents Make in Pursuit of Maths Excellence	
1	Neglecting Early Maths Practise
2	Lack of Belief in Your Child's Ability
3	Not Understanding 'Why'
4	Not Showing That Maths Matters and Skipping Daily Practise
5	Insufficient Practise
6	Sole Reliance on School Practise
7	Total Dependence on Tutors
8	Lack of Strong Fundamentals
9	Neglecting to Review Previously Learned Material
10	Rushing Through Problems and Neglecting Details
11	Hesitating to Seek Professional Help

Now that we know these common mistakes, just check which ones you need to work on. Once you know, overcoming these mistakes is crucial for your child's maths success. The *S-9 Framework* will be your guide and help you find and implement the solutions to these common mistakes that hinder your child's progress. With determination and consistent effort, your child can achieve maths success and open doors to a bright future.

Chapter 1.2

Achieving Maths Excellence with the S-9 Framework

As parents, we want nothing but the best for our children. We aspire to see them excel in their academics and beyond. However, the road to achieving a perfect score can be daunting in any subject, especially maths (but maths is the only subject where scoring 100/100 is possible), leaving you feeling helpless and overwhelmed. But fear not; neither you nor your child is alone on this journey. I am here to guide you toward your child's academic success in maths.

Using the *S-9 Framework,* you will find answers to the problems you have been facing. You can help your children overcome obstacles and achieve their full potential while creating a **lifelong love for learning.**

The *S-9 Framework* is a simple **9-step plan** to make maths more manageable for your child. With regular practise, it helps build a strong maths foundation and score well. The framework covers everything from having a positive attitude to effective study methods. It suggests starting with small steps, setting achievable goals, and celebrating successes. By using this approach, your child gains confidence and moves towards excellence. The framework also helps you, as a parent, actively participate in your child's education by providing practical solutions for busy schedules. It focuses on understanding your child's unique needs, promotes a positive mindset, and makes learning enjoyable.

I promise every parent and guardian reading this book that if you follow the *S-9 Framework* and walk on this journey with me, *this book will fill the gap between where your child is and where your child can be* without being overwhelmed and in chaos. This framework is the link that will help you take actionable steps to guide your child toward mastering maths.

Fig 1.2.1 *Maths Mastery: Bridging the Gap From Where You Are to Where You Want to Be*

Throughout this book, we will explore each element of the *S-9 Framework* in detail. By implementing these strategies in your child's life, you will witness remarkable transformations in their maths skills and overall academic performance. Together, we will create a roadmap to success, ensuring your child's ability to score to get good scores.

The curiosity that brought you here is the same curiosity that will drive you forward. Imagine the satisfaction you will feel when your child solves complex maths problems, understands concepts effortlessly, and achieves good scores. The *S-9 Framework* offers to make this dream a reality. It provides a clear path to follow, eliminating any confusion or uncertainty.

So, don't waste another moment. Take action now and embrace the power of the *S-9 Framework*. Equip yourself with the tools and knowledge to help your children reach their full potential in maths. Start your transformative journey towards becoming the proud parent of a maths genius today!

SECTION 2

STEPS FOR ACHIEVING MATHS EXCELLENCE

Chapter 2.1

S1: Set a Goal

> *"Whether you think you can, or think you can't... you're right."* – *Henry Ford*

I have worked with several parents who have all had the same goal of wanting their child to score 100/100 in maths. Many have expressed frustration and confusion about not knowing how to achieve this goal. Some have been so disheartened that they started calling it a dream, not a goal. However, I want to assure all parents that this goal is indeed achievable, and the first step towards reaching it is to **Set a Goal.**

Setting a goal starts with a belief. As a parent, you play a vital role in your child's academic success. So, parents, first **you** need to **believe** that your child can get a 100 out of 100 in maths. It might have seemed impossible before, but believe me, parents, it is possible—all you need to do is *believe in yourself and your child.*

You might think, *"Is it okay to set such a big goal? Am I putting too much pressure on my child?"*

This is when we start walking the wrong path. Goals aren't about stress. Setting a specific goal with your child can be a powerful motivator. You are both more likely to feel a sense of accountability. That can increase your commitment to achieving it and help you both stay on track and overcome obstacles. Setting a goal is like drawing a route on a map. It helps you and your child see the path you should take and the destination you aim to reach.

Setting a goal encourages individuals to put in more effort to achieve it. When a parent sets a goal, and their child puts effort towards achieving it, it results in **goal-directed behaviour, persistence, planning, and self-reflection.** When your child has a clear goal, it becomes easier for them to prioritise their time and efforts and know exactly what they need to work towards to achieve this goal. This will help them stay on track and avoid distractions, ensuring that they are making progress toward their goal.

In setting and achieving this goal, your child is more likely to confront and overcome their fears of failure and develop a more resilient approach to setbacks and obstacles. This *growth mindset* will help your child embrace challenges as opportunities to learn and grow.

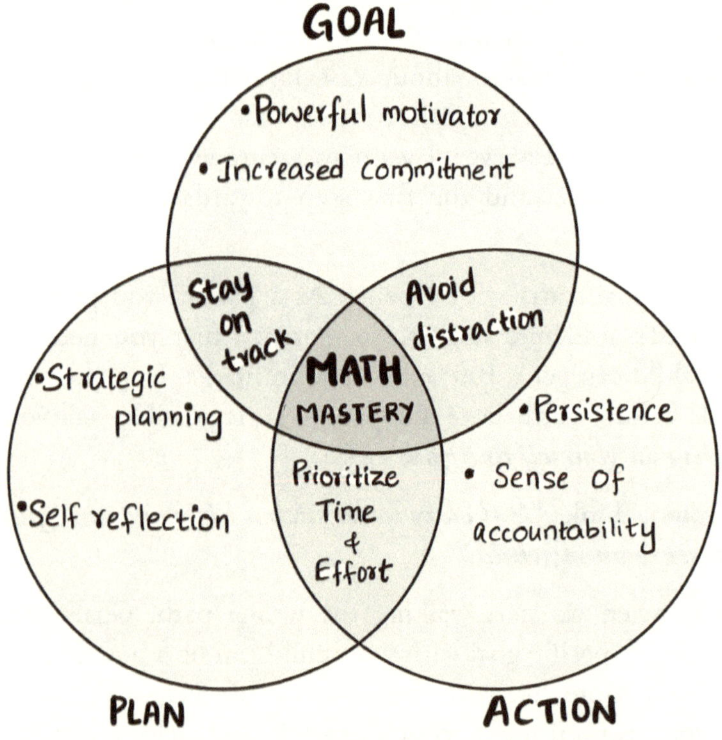

Fig 2.1.1 *Advantages of Goal Setting: Your First Step to Success*

Activity 2.1:

First things first, let's set a goal together. Research has shown that when goals are **written down** and **visualised**, they become more powerful and achievable. So, grab a poster or a piece of paper and prepare to make some magic happen. Let's do an exciting activity that brings joy and has a proven track record of success.

Step 1: Write these magical words:

YOU'RE A MATH GENIUS!

YOU HAVE SCORED 100/100 IN MATH!

Fig 2.1.2

Wait, there's more!

Step 2: Add your child's photo to the poster to make it even more awesome. It's like creating a personalised victory trophy to inspire and motivate you and your child.

Now, here's the fascinating part. Studies have shown that when parents actively participate in their children's academic goals, the chances of success skyrocket. By setting a goal with your child and working towards it together, you create a powerful support system that boosts their confidence and determination.

YOU'RE A MATH GENIUS!

YOU HAVE SCORED   /   IN MATH!

Fig 2.1.3

A digital copy of this worksheet can also be found in the Resource Bundle mentioned in the Introduction Section.

Step 3: Now, let's stick that incredible poster somewhere visible, like the fridge, bedroom wall, or study table. When children see their goals every day, it helps them stay focused and motivated. Every time you and your child see it, it will remind you both of the fantastic journey you're on together and the amazing things your child is capable of.

Fig 2.1.4 *Written Goals: Seeing Them Makes You Achieve Them*

In conclusion, setting a goal with your child to achieve 100/100 in maths is a great way to motivate and encourage them to improve their maths skills and achieve academic success. By providing motivation, clear focus, increased effort, a growth mindset, and accountability, setting a goal can help your child reach their full potential and achieve their academic goals. So, go ahead and put the goal together and work towards it with your child.

Remember, setting a goal is just the first step. The key to success lies in believing in your child's potential and taking action. Together, you can conquer any challenge (in Maths or Life) that comes your way!

Let me tell you an incredible story about a mom named Nimisha and her daughter, Aanya. Nimisha had a particular goal for Aanya – to score a perfect 100/100 in maths. Nimisha was determined to help Aanya achieve this goal but wasn't sure how to do it.

So, Nimisha and I worked together to make a plan using the *S-9 Framework*. We started with the first step, i.e., setting specific goals for Aanya's maths scores. Having a clear target made it easier for Nimisha to guide and encourage Aanya.

During the discussion, we decided to make Aanya's achievements even more exciting. As discussed, Nimisha created a colourful poster, saying, "Congratulations, Aanya! You're a Maths Star! You scored a perfect 100/100 in Maths!" Nimisha even added Aanya's photo to the poster.

This poster became a daily reminder for both Nimisha and Aanya of the goal they were working towards. Every time they looked at it, they felt motivated.

Months went by, and something extraordinary happened. Aanya's grades improved, and she scored a perfect 100/100 in maths, Aanya felt proud of herself.

Nimisha knew the poster had played a big part in Aanya's success. It reminded them of their goals and showed Aanya that her hard work was paying off. The poster became a symbol of Aanya's achievement, and it added even more value to her success.

P.S. If you like, you can start setting smaller goals for your child. These goals should be a little higher than what your child is scoring right now. It's a way to help them keep improving, step by step. So, whether it's aiming for 20 out of 25, 60 out of 80, or 80 out of 100, setting these goals can guide your child's progress in maths.

Once they achieve the goal you have set, you can replace the goal chart with a new one, set even higher than the one before. This gradual increase will help your child continuously challenge themselves and improve their maths skills.

So, parents, let's draw inspiration from Nimisha. Set goals with your children, help them create their Goal Chart, and celebrate their achievements. Believe that this will come true and let the power of goal setting start its work.

Chapter 2.2

S2: Strengths and Weaknesses – Identify Them

> *"Our strength grows out of our weaknesses." – Ralph Waldo Emerson*

Now that we are through with the first step, it's time to take the second – understanding your child's strengths and weaknesses.

Before I guide you through the activity, let's ensure we understand why identifying strengths and weaknesses is essential.

IDENTIFYING STRENGTHS AND WEAKNESSES IS REQUIRED.

Just like every child has unique abilities, they also possess *strengths* in maths. When you recognise and build upon these strengths, it boosts their confidence and motivation. It empowers them and instils a sense of belief in their capabilities. Furthermore, understanding your child's *weaknesses* is equally important. As a parent and their guide, you can comprehend the areas where they may encounter challenges. This understanding enables you to provide the required support, helping your child overcome these obstacles and enhance their performance in those areas.

2.2.1 *Why Identifying a Child's Strengths and Weaknesses Is Important*

This chapter covers gathering information about your child's strengths and weaknesses, and then using that information to create a plan to improve their maths skills and achieve the goal set in *Step 1*.

Sometimes, without realising it, parents may miss this vital step that can help their child succeed in maths. It may feel like a lot of effort, but trust me, it's worth it! Just like getting all the necessary tests done before starting a weight loss plan, understanding your child's strengths and weaknesses in maths is crucial for their progress. A study by the *National Council of Teachers of Mathematics (NCTM)* found that actively identifying and addressing students' strengths and weaknesses in maths leads to significant improvement.

The children whose parents help them set a goal, make a goal chart, and work with identifying their strengths and weaknesses tend to take more purposeful actions and make more informed decisions compared to those who only set the goal without action to understand their areas of improvement. Let's explore the findings and see how this can make a real difference.

Roles of a Parent	Parents Who Know Their Children's Strengths and Weaknesses	Parents Who Aren't Sure About Their Child's Strengths and Weaknesses
Setting Goals	They can help their children dream big and guide them.	They want their children to excel but aren't sure how.
Everyday Learning	They can plan their daily learning based on the topics their children need more support with.	They find it challenging to plan daily learning due to the uncertainty about their children's needs.
Providing Resources	They offer additional learning materials and seek out extra practise resources to support their children's studies.	They struggle to find suitable resources and guidance to aid their children's learning effectively.

Now that we understand the importance of knowing your child's strengths and weaknesses, do an activity to find these out.

Activity 2.2: The Maths Mastery Skills Assessment Chart

Let's look at this tool – the Maths Mastery Skills Assessment Chart. You can track your child's proficiency levels across various maths topics using this tool. This chart will help you understand your child's current skill level and identify areas where they may need extra attention.

Fig 2.2.2

Don't worry, parents. This chart might seem scary initially, but we'll guide you through it step by step. Grab a pencil and create your interactive Maths Mastery Skills Assessment Chart. Here's what you need to do:

Step 1: Break Down the Maths Curriculum.

Use the table above as a guide and add the following details:

Serial Number:	Write the numbers here. Start with 1 for the first topic, 2 for the second, and keep going.
Topic:	Write the maths lesson name, e.g., Addition, Subtraction, etc., that is relevant to your child as per age or grade.

Step 2: Sorting Your Child's Maths Skills

Collecting data in the correct format is crucial to ensure your children quickly reach their maths goals. Let's understand how you can identify the category your child belongs to: *Struggling, Need Practise, Good, Excellent, Accuracy, and Speed.*

Struggling	Put a tick (✔) if this topic is challenging for your child
Need Practise	Put a tick (✔) if your child should practise this topic more
Good	If your child knows this topic but not perfectly, put a tick (✔)
Excellent	If your child is very good at this topic, put a tick (✔)
Accuracy	If your child answers correctly most of the time, set a tick (✔)
Speed	If your child responds quickly and rightly, put a tick (✔)

Are you still feeling stuck? The chart can help you further:

If you still need help filling in the chart, don't worry! Here are a few easy steps:

a. ***Review Previous Test Results:*** See your child's past maths tests. If they keep making the same mistakes in a particular topic, this can tell you what they find challenging.

b. ***Talk to the Teachers:*** Talk to your child's class teacher. They can tell you about the areas where your child might need extra help.

c. ***Discuss the Mistakes with Your Child:*** Sit with your child and discuss the mistakes. You may ask them, *"Why do you think this went wrong?"* or *"How did you try to solve this?"* That can help you see what they understand and where they might get stuck.

d. ***Talk with Other Parents:*** Talking with other parents can give you new ideas. They may have found a helpful way to understand a few things better. Sharing thoughts and experiences can make things easier for everyone.

In my years of experience, I have encountered numerous heart-warming stories that highlight the power of strengths and weaknesses for effective teaching. Let me share one such story.

My engineering college friend, Swati, was worried about her son Aryan's struggles with maths. Aryan was feeling lost and frustrated regarding numbers, and she didn't know how to help him.

When Swati met me, she shared her concerns. Swati emphasised that she was good at maths and an engineer who deeply understood the importance of mathematical skills. Therefore, she wished for her son to excel in maths.

That's when I introduced her to this unique tool, the *Maths Mastery Skills Assessment Chart*.

Swati was excited about the skill chart and understood how it could help her Aryan. She started using the chart with him. It showed her what maths skills Aryan needed to work on and the areas he was doing well in.

With the *Maths Mastery Skills Assessment Chart* as their guide, Swati and Aryan began their maths-learning journey. They focused on the areas where Aryan needed help, practicing and doing exercises to strengthen those skills. Swati's dedication and Aryan's growing motivation created a positive learning environment, and Aryan started feeling more confident in maths.

As time went on, Swati could see the progress Aryan was making with the help of the skill chart. He gradually improved his maths skills and started doing well. Swati was so happy to see her efforts paying off. The skill chart gave her a sense of organisation and control over Aryan's maths education. She felt more confident as a parent.

Let me show you how the chart revealed which maths topic was easy for Aryan and which ones were a bit hard and how this chart guided Swati, turning things around for Aryan's maths journey.

MATHS MASTERY SKILLS ASSESSMENT CHART

Name: Aryan   Grade: 8   Date:

Srno	Topic	Understanding				Accuracy	Speed
		STRUGGLING	NEED PRACTISE	GOOD	EXCELLENT		
1	Addition			✓		✓	✓
2	Subtraction		✓				
3	Multiplication			✓		✓	
4	Division		✓				
5	Fractions		✓				
6	Percentages			✓		✓	✓

Fig 2.2.3

Here's what we found from the chart:

Topics	Comments
Addition	Good, mostly accurate, and fast.
Subtraction	Needs more practise.
Multiplication	Good and mostly accurate but not necessarily fast.
Division	Struggling with this topic.
Fractions	Finding this difficult and needs more practise.
Percentages	Proficient, accurate, and able to solve problems quickly.

Swati and Aryan's story shows that this chart is beneficial. It worked as a guide for Swati, who then used it to help Aryan. And the best thing? She was pleased to see Aryan get b etter at maths.

Their success story demonstrates the importance of using helpful tools and strategies to support our children's education. With the right resources and a structured approach, you can guide your children and give them the confidence they need to succeed in maths and beyond.

Before moving on to the next chapter, I suggest you have the first draft of this chart ready so that you can feel empowered, as Swati and the other parents did after using it.

Now that you have prepared the chart, some of you might be eager to start immediately, while others might still have questions or feel unsure about how to use it. Whatever you're feeling, I recommend reading the next chapter first. It will guide you on how to use and make the most of the chart.

Chapter 2.3

S3: Strong Foundation – Start Building

> *"Learning mathematics is a highly sequential process. If you miss out on fundamental aspects, the next stage cannot really be learned."*
> *- Keith Devlin*

Congratulations, parents! You have taken the first two steps towards helping your child become a maths superstar!

Now that you've figured out your child's *strengths* and *weaknesses* using the *Maths Skills Assessment Chart*, it's time to make a plan and start working on it. But before that, don't forget about those strong fundamentals! You need to begin with the basics—the most straightforward stuff—so that your child can feel like a champion right from the start. It might not be the most exciting part, but trust me, it's super important.

Let's consider building a house for a moment. When we build a home, we don't rush to build the walls or the roof without a solid foundation, right? This foundation keeps the whole house sturdy and safe. Well, the same goes for maths! We want to ensure your child's maths skills have a solid foundation so they can tackle more challenging problems as they grow.

I understand that sometimes children aren't too thrilled about maths. They might find it hard or get frustrated easily. But that's where you need to step in to help! Focusing on those basic skills can boost your child's confidence and make maths way more enjoyable. Trust me, when they feel like maths superheroes, they'll actually start to like it!

Now, let's talk about why working with your child to build a strong foundation will help them gain confidence and develop a love for maths.

Feeling Like a Champion:

Starting with the easy stuff can immediately make your child feel like they're winning. As they master these basic skills, they'll feel proud and motivated to take on more challenging concepts.

Boosts their Confidence:

Starting with the fundamentals and mastering both accuracy and speed will help your child tackle maths problems and find solutions faster, boosting their confidence. That means higher scores and better performance!

Making Maths Exciting:

As your child gains confidence, they'll start to like maths more. They'll be more curious, ask questions, and actively participate in class. That will lead to a deeper understanding and a real passion for maths.

Long-term Success:

With a strong maths foundation and the right skills to handle anything that comes their way, they will be ready to face more challenging maths concepts in their school. Slowly, this will help them with tests and future academic adventures.

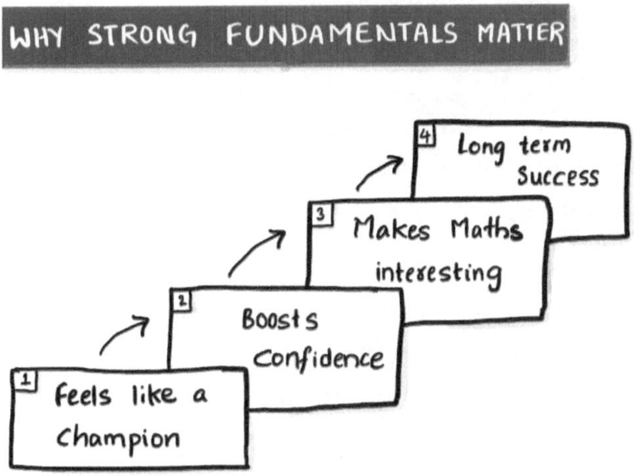

Fig 2.3.1 *Why Strong Fundamentals Matter*

Activity 2.3:

From the *Maths Mastery Skill Assessment Chart* that we got in *Step 2*, we will now consider aspects like speed, accuracy, and understanding. Following this, we will choose a topic that is most fundamental where the child just needs a little practise or needs to improve speed. Then, together with your child, let's improve their performance.

Step 1: We'll begin by focusing on speed. Find a topic that your child knows well and is accurate in, but needs to get quicker.

Step 2: Once they get faster on that point, we'll move on to topics they understand but need to be more accurate at before they focus on speed.

Step 3: Finally, we'll take the rest of the topics, one after another, ensuring they understand them well, work on their accuracy, and then on speed. This way, they'll gradually improve in them all and develop their maths skills.

Example: If they struggle with multiplication, aim to increase their speed and accuracy this month. Remember, the journey is as important as the destination!

Aditi, a devoted parent, approached me with concerns about her daughter, Riya, and her struggle with fractions. Upon conducting a comprehensive assessment using the *Maths Mastery Skills Assessment Chart*, it became clear that Riya's weak foundation in multiplication tables slowed her progress across various mathematical areas. I shared these findings with Aditi, who was determined to support Riya in every way possible.

Aditi and I devised a plan to strengthen Riya's multiplication skills. Aditi's commitment and active involvement substantially impacted Riya's learning journey. As she got better at multiplications, her understanding of fractions improved. As her marks improved, she became more confident.

Another parent, Sunaina, also sought my guidance regarding her child, Shiv, and his struggles with fractions. After creating the *Maths Mastery Skills Assessment Chart*, it became evident that Shiv's weak grasp of multiplication tables was hindering his progress. I shared this insight with Sunaina, emphasising the crucial role of addressing this fundamental skill.

However, Sunaina had doubts, considering multiplication tables were too easy for Shiv. She believed that focusing on high-level concepts would yield more significant benefits. Sunaina continued with her current approach, disregarding the essential foundation of multiplication.

Over time, the contrasting approaches taken by Aditi and Sunaina yielded noticeable results. While Riya did well under Aditi's dedicated support, Shiv continued to face challenges in fractions due to his weak multiplication skills.

Sunaina soon realised that not focusing on multiplication had kept Shiv from doing his best.

Sunaina's journey from doubt to becoming an advocate for foundational skills was not easy. She initially felt a sense of concern and sadness while witnessing Shiv's struggles with fractions. However, after observing the positive impact of Aditi's approach with Riya, she decided to share her worries with Aditi.

Aditi attentively listened to Sunaina's concerns and recounted her experience of guiding Riya through a similar journey. She shared how mastering the basics of multiplications had helped Riya perform better in other maths topics as well. Aditi's sincere sharing helped Sunaina see things differently.

Sunaina approached me again, putting more trust in my guidance and the importance of getting the basics right. Together, we developed a focused plan to strengthen Shiv's multiplication skills. Sunaina committed herself to helping Shiv improve his multiplication abilities. She started engaging with him in regular practise sessions. With Sunaina's active involvement, Shiv's confidence and understanding of fractions improved significantly. He began to excel in his maths assessments, experiencing a newfound joy in learning. Witnessing Shiv's growing passion for maths, increased confidence, and enhanced performance, filled Sunaina's heart with immense pleasure and pride.

As a parent, witnessing your child develop a genuine love for maths and gain confidence in their abilities is an incredibly fulfilling experience. Sunaina's happiness and pride in Shiv's progress are a powerful testament to embracing foundational skills and actively participating in your child's maths education.

I've heard many talks between parents and their children. I know it's hard when you try to teach the basic things, and your child doesn't want to listen. But these challenging times will help your child succeed in life.

For the parents who've taken the step and completed this exercise – your dedication shines brightly, and we truly appreciate your efforts for your child's future. For those who are still thinking, remember to trust the process and take that step.

If you need a little nudge and convincing to do the exercise, let me walk you through a simple conversation between a parent and the child. It will show why building a solid foundation now is crucial for their future. I hope by sharing this, parents will feel encouraged and know that they're not the only ones working hard for their child's promising future.

Reshma watched her daughter Maahika struggle with her maths homework. It pained her to see Maahika getting frustrated over algebra problems. Wanting to help, Reshma approached her.

Reshma: "Maahika, I see you're struggling with maths. Would you like to talk about it?"

Maahika: "Oh, Mum, maths is so boring! I keep doing the sums repeatedly, and they come out wrong. I don't want to do it."

Reshma: "I get it, sweetie. But I looked into how I can help you. Guess what I found out?"

Maahika: "What?"

Reshma: "I filled out this *Maths Mastery Skills Assessment Chart* and discussed it with a professional who suggested something important. Your basics, like multiplication, need some work. It might sound boring, but getting good at that will make algebra easier."

Maahika: "I know multiplication, Mum! What is the use of doing it again and again?"

Reshma: "Remember when you learned to cycle? At first, it was tricky and you were slow but you got so good with practise. Maths is like that. If you know your multiplication tables on your fingertips, you can solve maths problems quicker and more easily, and feel more confident. And guess what? We can make it fun!"

Maahika: "Fun? How?"

Reshma: "We can do maths every day for just 15 minutes. We can also play maths games, have little contests, and make it exciting. I'm here with you in this."

Maahika: "Ok, Mum. Let's try!"

Over the days, Reshma and Maahika practised maths along with games and laughter. They turned learning maths into a fun adventure with every possible opportunity they got.

Reshma: "What is 7 times 8?"

> Maahika: "56!"
>
> Reshma: "Well done, my champion! What is 9 times 4?"
>
> Maahika: "36!"
>
> Soon, Maahika began to see a change.
>
> While Reshma was preparing breakfast one morning, Maahika approached her with a wide smile.
>
> Maahika: "Mom, with all the practise we've been doing, I struggled with multiplication tables, but now they come to me naturally. And you know what? Algebra doesn't scare me anymore."
>
> Reshma: "See? I knew you could do it. And I'm so proud of how hard you tried."
>
> Reshma's heart swelled with pride, seeing the transformation in her child. They had come a long way together, overcoming challenges and embracing the beauty of maths.
>
> With Reshma's help, Maahika learned that starting with simple things in maths made the complicated stuff more accessible. When you get the basics right, everything else becomes simpler.

While the journey may seem challenging initially, remember that you're not alone, and the results are gratifying. But the journey doesn't stop here. It's crucial to go to the next step, S4, and create a *Study Planner* to track your child's progress and improvement. By monitoring their progress, you can adjust this plan as required.

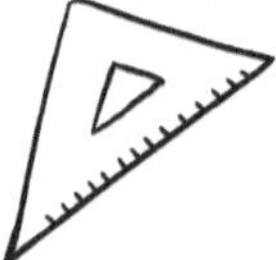

Chapter 2.4

S4: Study Planner – Track and Stay Organised

> *"A goal without a plan is just a wish." – Antoine de Saint-Exupéry*

So, parents, we've set a goal, looked at what your child is good at and what they need help with, and picked the topics to focus on. Now, what's next? In this chapter, we'll learn how to watch. Observe how your child is doing in these topics and find ways to help them do even better. Curious about how this can be done? Let's find out together!

You will now create a *Study Planner* for tracking your child's progress, as it is an essential step towards achieving success. As parents, it is crucial to follow your child's daily study planner to ensure they are making progress toward their academic goals.

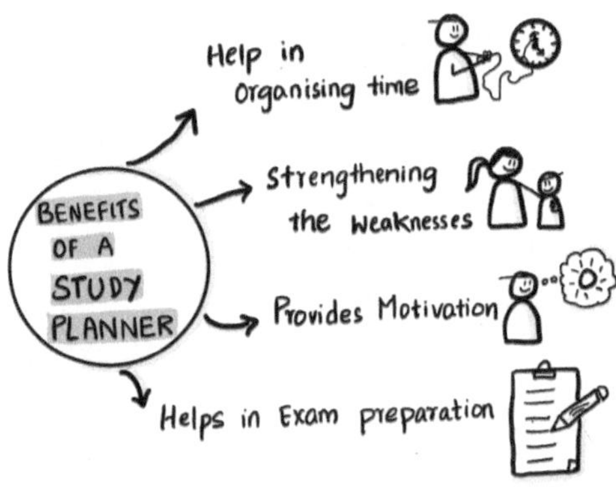

Fig 2.4.1

We can see that tracking your child's progress using a Study Planner is essential to achieving success in mathematics. You can track it daily, weekly, and monthly to ensure they are making progress towards their academic goals.

Creating a study planner and staying organised to keep track of your child's educational journey can often feel overwhelming. Hence, with my experience, I have meticulously designed *"The Maths Mastery Study Planner"* to simplify this process. This planner, an integral part of the *S-9 framework*, is crafted especially for dedicated parents like you. *The Maths Mastery Study Planner* isn't just any planner. It's a roadmap tailored to help you track your child's progress, ensuring you're always in tune with their progress and needs.

Instead of just talking about its potential, let us experience it first-hand by doing the next activity. This hands-on activity will familiarise you with its features and make you a pro in tracking and guiding your child's academic endeavours. By the end of it, you'll see why *The Maths Mastery Study Planner* isn't just a tool but an ally in your child's educational journey.

Activity 2.4:

If you do not have a pencil, please grab it and let's get started.

MATHS MASTERY STUDY PLANNER

Name: Grade:

Date	Topic	No. of Problems Solved	No. of Problems Correct	Time Taken	Mastery Level (1 to 10)	Remarks

Fig 2.4.2

Instructions To Fill The
STUDY PLANNER

Field	How To Fill
Date	Write when your child is working on the problems.
Topic	Note down what topic your child is working on. For example: Addition, Multiplication, or Logarithms etc.
No of Problems Solved	Count and write how many problems or questions your child finished.
Number of Problems Correct	Count how many answers your child got right.
Time Taken	Check the clock before starting and after finishing. Write how long your child took.
Mastery Level (1-10)	Think about how well your child did. If they found it easy, write a number close to 10. If it was hard, write a number closer to 1
Remarks:	Write any extra notes here. Like if your child finds something hard or easy or needs more practise.

Let us look at a sample study planner and then you can start making yours.

MATHS MASTERY
STUDY PLANNER

Name: Grade:

Date	Topic	No. of Problems Solved	No. of Problems Correct	Time Taken	Mastery Level (1 to 10)	Remarks
1/5	Multiplication	50	35	25	4	Can do better
2/5	Multiplication	50	40	20	8	Need a little more practise on 8 tables
3/5	Multiplication	50	48	15	9	Can go ahead with the next topic
4/5	Division	50	30	25	3	Stuggling
5/5	Division	50	35	22	6	Can do better
6/5	Division	50	45	16	9	Can go ahead with the next topic

As seen from the above sample study planner, encourage your child to practise maths problems daily, and you can record their progress in the corresponding cells. This way, you can identify the number of questions they completed and the time spent practising. After each practise session, you can assess their understanding and assign a mastery level based on their confidence and accuracy.

This format allows you to track their progress in different maths topics. It also helps you reflect on their strengths and areas that may need further practise or improvement. Feel free to modify the format based on the specific maths topics your child is studying and add any additional columns or categories that you find relevant or helpful.

This is just the beginning. As you keep doing this regularly, you can slowly and gradually encourage your child to continue and you can monitor it. This way, your child can start understanding, self-assessing their performance, and tracking their progress.

The beauty of this scheduler is that you can initially track your child's maths performance, but going forward, you can use a similar scheduler for any subject you want them to excel in.

Transforming Your Child's Mindset With
STUDY PLANNER

Before Tracking Progress	While Tracking Progress
They're unsure: They need a clear target in mind.	They have clear goals: They know the goals they want to achieve.
They might waste time: They might spend time on things they already know.	They use their time wisely: They spend time where it's needed.
They hesitate: They might need to realise when and where they need help.	They ask for help: When they find something challenging, they ask for help.
They might get discouraged: Losing hope is easy without a clear view of their progress.	They stay excited: Seeing their progress keeps them motivated.

In a 5th-grade class, two moms stood out: Ayan's mother and Arshi's mom. They both wanted their children to get perfect scores in maths, but their methods were different.

Ayan's mother loved the *S-9 Framework*. She saw the value of a structured approach. She didn't just set goals for Ayan, she also used *The Maths Mastery Study Planner*. With this planner, she tracked Ayan's progress and checked his assignments and practise exercises. Understanding his strengths and weaknesses allowed her to focus on areas needing more attention. They noted the maths problems that were tricky for Ayan. Each evening, they reviewed how he did, noting his successes, and areas needed for further practise. With this structure, Ayan's test scores improved. Slowly but gradually, he started scoring full marks in all his maths exams.

Arshi, on the other hand, struggled with her maths. She wanted to do better, but without a clear plan, she did not know what to focus on. Without the *S-9 Framework*, she was often unsure of the way forward. This left her feeling frustrated and disheartened.

At a parent-teacher meeting, Ayan's mother told Arshi's mom about the *S-9 Framework* and the *Maths Mastery Study Planner*. Arshi's mom saw its potential and decided to try it. Arshi and her mother began to identify her strong and weak areas, set clear goals, and regularly reviewed her progress. Over time, Arshi's maths skills and confidence grew and she started scoring well.

The impact of following the *Maths Mastery Study Planner* is evident in the above case study. Arshi's mother, though started late, recognised the significance of these steps and observed positive changes in Arshi's learning journey.

Dear parents, this underscores that your active involvement in tracking your child's progress using the *Maths Mastery Study Planner* can significantly influence their academic growth. Initially, you will need to put some effort into this, but gradually, you will see that your child will become independent. Setting clear goals and tracking progress empowers them to stay motivated, overcome challenges, and reach their true potential. Remember, a bit of planning combined with the guidance of the study planner, can make a world of difference in your child's education.

Chapter 2.5

S5: Silly Mistakes – Focus and Review

> *"The greatest mistake you can make in life is to be continually fearing you will make one." – Elbert Hubbard*

Now that you've incorporated the *Maths Mastery Study Planner* and observed your child's progress, you may have noticed they're making mistakes. Despite their best efforts, these errors in their maths studies can be both frustrating and demotivating for you and your child.

However, there's a silver lining. Think back to when your child was learning to walk. Remember those countless stumbles and falls? It might have taken weeks or even months for them to master it. Nevertheless, with every fall, they learned something new, and you, as parents, never gave up. You knew the importance of walking and continued to guide and support them, sometimes holding their hand, and at other times, watching from a distance, but always present.

In this academic journey of mathematics, there will be similar challenges. While learning maths, it's normal for children to make mistakes, however silly they may be, and they're essential for improving. *Stanford University's Carol Dweck* studied why it's important to keep trying when learning. Her research shows that when students see mistakes as chances to learn, they do better in maths. She found that when students believe they can learn and improve if they keep trying, they do better in maths. So, let's teach our students that mistakes are just a part of the journey to becoming good at maths. Let's acknowledge that it's okay to make mistakes and encourage them to keep trying. Just as you wouldn't scold your child for falling while learning to walk, it's essential to approach their maths mistakes with the same patience and understanding.

Now that you know every wrong answer or complex problem in maths is a chance to learn, you need to guide your children. By helping your children understand their mistakes and looking at them positively together, you can find areas needing more attention and give them the skills to solve similar problems confidently later.

Recognising the reason for the mistakes is vital.

Understanding why your child is making mistakes is now vital. It might be easy to think, "*My child isn't good at maths*" or ignore mistakes as "*silly*", but finding the real cause is how we find lasting solutions.

We can categorise the reasons for your child's mistakes while doing maths as follows:

  i. *External Challenges*: Relate to understanding or skills, such as a missed calculation step.

  ii. *Internal Challenges*: These encompass personal challenges like self-doubt or fear of failure.

You need to identify the root cause of the problem and why your child is making mistakes to ensure your efforts to address the issue yield the desired results. Let's understand each of these a little more.

i. External Challenges:

External problems typically stem from:

  a. *Understanding Issues:* If your child has difficulty understanding a concept, reaching out for help or support is essential. Teachers, tutors, or professionals can provide clarity.

  b. *Accuracy Issues:* Regular practise can help your child improve accuracy. (Details in Chapters 2.6).

While addressing these external problems, you may realise that these are not the only issues your child is dealing with. Your child might also face internal challenges, as described below.

ii. Internal Challenges:

Many students secretly desire and wish that they should be good at maths, and also get a perfect score, but because they feel incapable, they might say, *"I do not like Maths"* or *"Maths isn't my subject."*

It's unfortunate to see child doubting their abilities. They might get upset and feel like they can't do something. Dealing with these internal issues is essential as sometimes, not feeling confident can hide a child's true potential.

Addressing your child's internal problems is often more critical than dealing with the external ones. If you only address the external issues, the child might continue feeling frustrated. Identifying and resolving the root cause of their frustration can significantly change their attitude and performance.

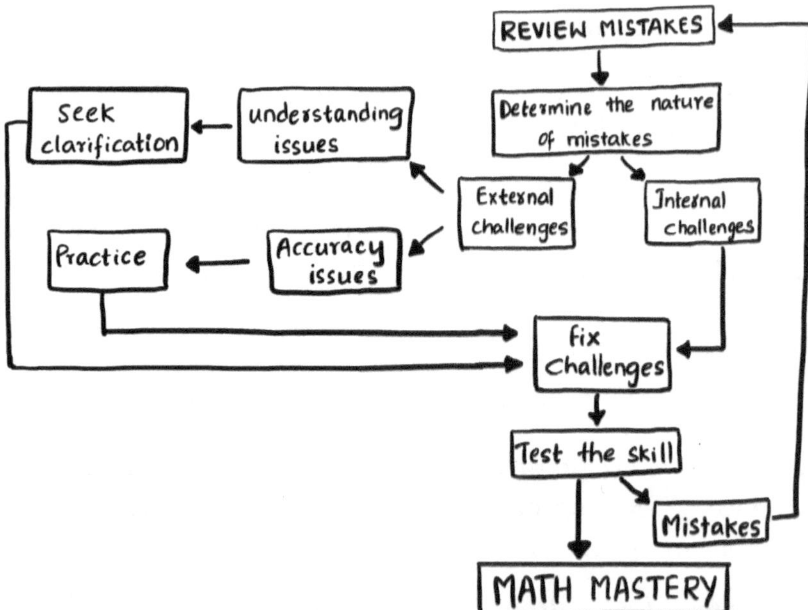

Fig 2.5.1 *Root Cause Analysis Flowchart: Understanding Child's Mistakes*

Anil always noticed that his son, Viraj, struggled with *Simultaneous Equations*. Every time they sat down to study, Anil observed Viraj making the same mistakes, like interchanging the signs. Initially, Anil thought these were just careless errors on Viraj's part. "It's a silly mistake," he'd say, thinking it might just be a lack of focus.

However, when Anil's colleague mentioned the *S-9 Framework* and how it can help Anil, he decided to try it. Anil and Viraj went through the framework step by step and started analysing the reasons for the mistakes instead of merely correcting them. They wanted to know why the errors were repeatedly happening.

By closely examining Viraj's work, Anil realised that the root of the problem wasn't merely "silly mistakes". Viraj needed a more fundamental understanding of certain concepts. He needed clarification about what rules to apply and when. This lack of clarity led him to interchange the signs.

But there was another layer to the problem. As Anil discussed the mistakes, Viraj confessed, "Dad, sometimes I feel like I'm not good enough." This internal challenge—a lack of self-belief—combined with his external challenges made maths a daunting subject for him.

Empowered with this insight from the *S-9 Framework*, Anil began to address both challenges. They revisited the basics of simultaneous equations, ensuring Viraj understood the foundational concepts. Anil sought extra resources and sometimes even approached the teachers to help clarify Viraj's doubts.

Equally important, Anil worked on boosting Viraj's confidence. They celebrated small victories, and Anil constantly reminded his son that everyone learns at their own pace and mistakes were a part of the journey.

Soon, a transformation occurred. As Viraj's understanding deepened and his confidence grew, his performance in maths improved drastically. His school teachers began to notice this change. Viraj started receiving appreciation for his remarkable turnaround, and his confidence soared even higher.

Anil felt a profound sense of pride. The *S-9 Framework* helped him guide Viraj academically and strengthened their bond as father and son. Viraj's newfound confidence became a testament to their joint effort and the power of understanding the root causes of challenges.

This case study illustrates the journey of a parent and child in overcoming academic difficulties through understanding, patience, and the proper guidance, making it relatable for many parents. Once we understand the exact problem, addressing it will become easy and progress will follow.

The *S-9 Framework's* power lies in its holistic approach. It doesn't just aim for a perfect score; it focuses on the enthusiasm and confidence a child feels when they achieve their goals. *Chapter 2* concentrates entirely on the *External Challenges*. We will discuss the *Internal Challenges* in *Chapter 3*.

Chapter 2.6

S6: Similar Problems – Practise, Practise, Practise

> *"I've missed over 9000 shots in my career. I've lost almost 300 games. 26 times, I've been trusted to take the game-winning shot and missed. I've failed over and over and over again in my life. And that is why I succeed." – Michael Jordan*

Once you have identified the challenges discussed in *Chapter 2.5* and the pattern of your child's mistakes, the next important step is to fix them by practising similar problems.

WHY PRACTISE MATTERS?

Children must practise every topic thoroughly to strengthen their foundational knowledge in maths. With numerous topics and rules to learn, repetition is vital. Without regular practise, concepts might be forgotten over time, leading to confusion. Think of maths learning like swimming: simply watching videos or studying the theory isn't enough; the hands-on experience of diving in and trying it is essential. Similarly, understanding mistakes alone isn't sufficient for our children; active practise is necessary for improvement.

WHY PRACTISE MATTERS

Field	How To Fill
Better Understanding	Daily practise helps your child remember maths better, ensuring a solid grasp of topics.
Improved Accuracy	Regular problem-solving enhances understanding and reduces mistakes
Enhanced Retention	Consistent practise aids in long-term retention.
Improves Speed	Daily practise increases speed in problem-solving, allowing for quicker responses.
Increased Confidence	Regular problem-solving boosts confidence and reduces test anxiety.
Getting Ready for Exams	Daily maths practise improves test-taking skills, including time management and clear thinking.
Better Grades	More practise leads to better marks enhancing overall academic performance.

Fig 2.6.1 *The Importance of Writing Practise*

Many of us remember when practise meant jotting down notes or writing solutions step by step. In today's digital age, this essence of writing might need to be re-discovered. But don't forget, there's more to practise than just oral repetition. Practise involves writing out solutions step by step. Parents often say that despite covering the entire syllabus, their child doesn't score well in exams. You and your child might think they understand a concept because they can answer questions orally. However, without writing it down, they falter in written exams. The reason? Lack of written practise. More often than not, the missing link is written practise. When children write, they engage differently, and this active engagement is often the key to retaining and applying knowledge.

Consistent Practise vs. Rote Learning

We all want the best for our kids. Some of us fear that daily practise leads to rote learning or mechanical memorisation. But let's differentiate between the two. Daily practise is about understanding, internalising, and then mastering the topic to the point where your child can confidently tackle any related question, even if woken up in the middle of the night. Remember the earlier example of how we still recite nursery rhymes from our childhood? We still know them because we repeated them regularly. The same principle applies to maths; practising problems daily embeds mathematical concepts into a child's memory. That's the power of repetition combined with understanding.

Like all the other students, Nidhi, who was in Grade 3, used her fingers to add numbers.

However, with time, she began changing her approach. She started visualising numbers in her mind rather than relying on her fingers. This shift made her faster in answering. Soon, she could instantly provide answers, not just for addition but also for subtraction and multiplication.

Her teachers noticed this and were surprised at how fast she could calculate and answer while the other kids were still thinking. They wanted to know how. So, they talked to Nidhi's mom and dad.

Nidhi's parents shared their experience with their older child, who had difficulties with maths. And how, after much trial and error and research, they discovered the *S-9 Framework*. They expressed how this framework helped their elder one develop her maths concepts, bridging her gaps in understanding. As they did not want Nidhi to have the same problem, they were determined to give Nidhi a head start. Hence, they introduced her to the method suggested by the *S-9 Framework* before she faced any challenges. They ensured Nidhi practised writing maths daily, even if just for 15-20 minutes, and regularly posed random questions to her. They also set time challenges to boost her speed. This proactive approach led to a remarkable transformation in Nidhi's maths skills.

Nidhi's story is a happy one. It tells parents that with a good start and the right path, all kids can be good at maths, just like Nidhi.

There's power in what we do daily, like eating, sleeping, and brushing. Practising maths should also be a daily routine for your child. The more they practise, the better they'll get. Encouraging them to do maths problems daily helps them prepare for tests and perform well. Even if they don't get perfect scores right away, regular practise leads to improvement. So, ensure they practise daily to excel in school.

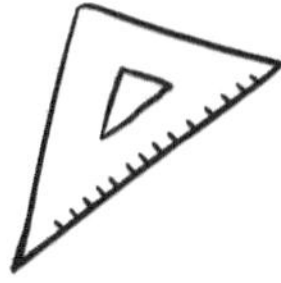

Chapter 2.7

S7: Study Scheduler – Develop Your Schedule

> *"Every minute you spend in planning, saves 10 minutes in execution; this gives you a 1,000 percent return on energy!" – Brian Tracy*

Parents, many of you might be feeling quite overwhelmed by now. The dream of seeing your child score well in their maths exam may seem like hard work, but every ounce of effort will be worth the outcome. Take a deep breath, and believe me when I say that scoring perfect marks is not unattainable.

S1: Gave us an idea of where we wanted to reach;

S2: Guided us with the road map;

S3: Showed us where to start the journey;

S4: How to follow the road map;

S5: Helped keep track if we got lost; and

S6: Guided us on whether we were doing it right.

Yet sometimes, despite all the hard work, the results might not meet expectations, leading to disappointment. But the fault might not be in your or your child's effort. It might lie in an ineffective study schedule. After going through years of experience and doing my research, I found the answer to the question:

WHY DO YOU NEED A STUDY SCHEDULER?

As a parent myself, I can't stress enough the importance of a study scheduler; you know its significance too. It helps your child manage time effectively, ensuring dedicated study sessions. The plan establishes consistency through regular study times, reinforcing learning and retention, and creates a sense of responsibility and accountability for you and your child.

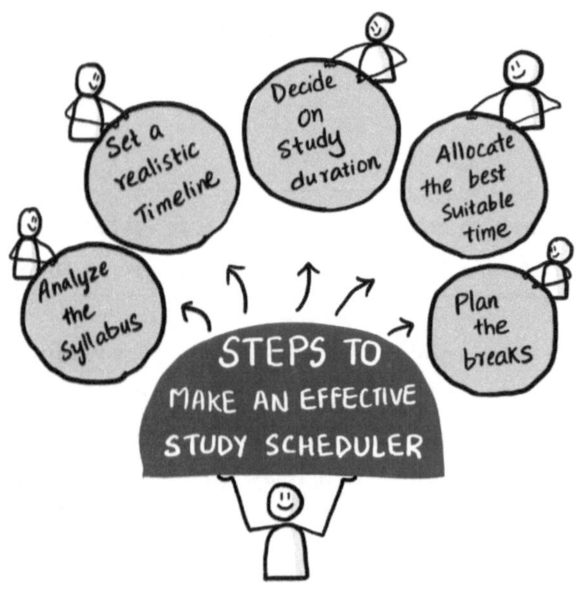

Fig 2.7.1

Before we proceed, I would like to share with you all the biggest challenge that parents usually express, when I start to discuss their child's study schedule.

> **Parent:** I don't have any fixed time to allocate for my child's studies. I'm always busy with work and other responsibilities. Plus, my child never seems to be able to sit down and study when free. My child is exhausted after school and has tuition; and only wants to play and watch TV. I'm at a loss. What can I do?

Do you also relate to this? Do you also find yourself facing similar struggles? If yes, you're not alone. Many parents experience the challenges of balancing work, household responsibilities, and their child's education. The good news is that you can implement strategies to overcome these obstacles and effectively plan your child's study schedule.

Planning for your child to practise maths in sync with their natural body rhythm is really important. This approach offers many benefits. The following guidelines help you explore possible solutions:

Study with the Sun:

Waking up early and studying within the first hour of the day is beneficial for aligning with the sun. Allocating 20 minutes each day for maths improvement is effective. Mornings are ideal for focused learning when both you and your child are fresh and energised. By waking up slightly earlier and dedicating those minutes to maths, you can efficiently utilise your time before daily commitments take over.

12 Hours Waking Window:

If mornings aren't suitable, consider a study session right after your child returns from school. If your child tackles their maths tasks immediately, they can later indulge in other activities without the weight of pending homework. Energy levels are usually high, allowing them to give their best. For instance, if they wake up at 7 am, aim to complete the maths practise by 7 pm, maximising the brain's peak 12-hour efficiency window.

No Late Nights:

Avoid late-night study sessions. By this time, the child is often too tired, diminishing their concentration levels. Striking a balance between relaxation and study is vital to avoid feeling overwhelmed. They might be able to study longer, but the quality needs to improve.

Remember, consistency is key. The human mind thrives on consistency. Even short, regular study sessions can make a significant impact over time. Studying at irregular times daily or frequently changing study times can exhaust the mind, leading to feelings of tiredness. During these times, make studying fun and interactive for your child. Let them know the importance of education, especially in improving their maths skills. A little effort every day can lead to great results over time.

Student A: Sarah

Sarah, a 6th-grader, aimed for a perfect score in maths. With her parents, she utilised the *S-9 Framework* to craft a personalised study schedule using the *Maths Mastery Study Scheduler*. This scheduler outlined the topics to cover, designated study times, and included breaks for relaxation. Sarah followed her schedule diligently, adjusting as necessary, with her trainer's guidance. By dedicating ample study time each day and taking regular breaks, she prepared effectively for exams and improved her grades. She soon started scoring 100/100 in her maths exams.

Student B: John

Similarly, determined to excel in maths, high school student, John also made a Study Scheduler. Despite creating a study schedule with his parents, John struggled to review or implement it consistently. Instead, he invested significant effort into exam preparation without a structured plan. Consequently, he became demotivated, lacked consistency in study efforts, and found it challenging to maintain focus during breaks. As a result, John's exam performance fell short of his expectations, resulting in a lower grade compared to Sarah's.

Comparison: The main difference between Sarah and John was how they planned their study time. Sarah followed a carefully made schedule with help from her trainer. This kept her focused and motivated. On the other hand, John didn't have a clear plan. This made it hard for him to manage his time well, stay motivated, and study effectively. Sarah's approach helped her study efficiently, while John struggled with motivation and wasted time on unproductive activities.

This case study shows that creating and following a study scheduler is crucial for achieving academic success. Students with a study scheduler can manage their time better, maintain consistency in their efforts, and stay motivated. Sarah's success in scoring well in maths is a testament to the importance of having a well-structured study scheduler.

Transforming Your Child's Mindset With

STUDY PLANNER

Students with a Study Scheduler	Students without a Study Scheduler
Know what to study when	Not sure when and where to start
Divide study time well	Might skip study sessions, avoid tasks
Feel responsible and motivated	Waste time deciding what to study
Use time well, balance study and rest	Feel stressed, no plan
Study regularly for better learning	Study times vary a lot, hard to keep up

Creating a study schedule doesn't mean turning your child into a robot. It's about instilling discipline while allowing flexibility. Encourage your child to take ownership of their study scheduler and give them some control over it. Be open to adjustments based on their needs and circumstances. Finding the right balance between discipline and flexibility will create a positive learning environment for your child. Finding the right study time for both of you might take some experimentation. Stay patient and flexible. With a good plan, your child can grow to love maths and do their best.

A good study scheduler works best with clear goals, a straightforward path, and is flexible. After going through years of experience and doing my research, I designed this simple yet very effective scheduler – the *Maths Mastery Daily Study Scheduler*. With the *Maths Mastery Study Planner* in place and a keen eye on your child's performance, it's time to chart out a *Maths Mastery Daily Study Scheduler*. This scheduler will help you with your child's daily study timeline. I suggest you sit with your child, discuss this scheduler, and dedicate daily time to maths, mainly focusing more on areas that need brushing up. So, let's fine-tune our approach, set realistic, achievable goals, and explore the steps to create such a study scheduler.

HOW TO MAKE AN EFFECTIVE STUDY SCHEDULER

1	Analyse the Syllabus	From Step 2, you've already reviewed your child's syllabus and have a list of topics. You also understand their strong and weak areas.
2	Set a Realistic Timeline	Building on Step 3, review the syllabus to identify the focus areas. Set clear timelines, breaking tasks into smaller parts with achievable deadlines.
3	Decide on the Study Duration	Decide how much time your child can devote to studying maths each day.
4	Allocate Time	Decide what time works best for your child. Aim to have them study at the same time each day. This establishes a routine, which can be beneficial.
5	Plan the Breaks	Help your child split their study time into shorter sessions, ensuring they take enough breaks.

Activity 2.7:

Step 1: Print two copies of this blank scheduler. This way, you'll grasp the importance and power of this scheduler.

MATHS MASTERY
STUDY SCHEDULER

Name: Grade: Date :

	MON	TUE	WED	THU	FRI	SAT	SUN
6:00 am							
6:00 - 7:00 am							
7:00 - 8:00 am							
8:00 - 9:00 am							
9:00 - 10:00 am							
10:00 - 11:00 am							
11:00 - 12:00 pm							
12:00 - 1:00 pm							
1:00 - 2:00 pm							
2:00 - 3:00 pm							
3:00 - 4:00 pm							
4:00 - 5:00 pm							
5:00 - 6:00 pm							
6:00 - 7:00 pm							
7:00 - 8:00 pm							
8:00 - 9:00 pm							
9:00 - 10:00 pm							

Step 2: Using a pencil, roughly outline your child's current schedule. If you need guidance, refer to the sample schedulers on the following pages to help you fill it in.

I've shared two sample study schedules for school students, each designed for different days – one for school days and one for no-school days. Subsequently, I've also combined them into a single sample study scheduler for your convenience.

MATHS MASTERY STUDY SCHEDULER
Sample For School Days

Time	Activity
6:00 am	Wake up
6:00 - 6:30 am	Get ready for school
6:30 -7:00 am	Practise math
7:00 am - 3:00 pm	Attend school
3:00 - 4:00 pm	Travel time. Relax. (BREAK)
4:00 - 4:30 pm	Quick bite (BREAK)
4:30 - 5:00 pm	Study maths - Topic 1
5:00 - 6:00 pm	Complete school homework and assignments
6:00 - 7:00 pm	Take a break. Relax and play
7:00 - 7:30 pm	Have dinner
7:30-8:00 pm	Play
8:30-9:00 pm	Prepare for the next day. Wind up and get ready for bed

MATH MASTERY STUDY SCHEDULER
Sample For No School Days

TIME	Activity
8:00 am	Wake up and finish morning Chores
9:00 am - 10:00 am	Practise Maths for 30 minutes
10:00 am - 11:00 am	Breakfast
11:00 am- 12:00 pm	Study Subject 1
12:00 - 3:00 pm	Have Lunch and Relax (BREAK)
3:00 - 4:00 pm	Study Subject 2
4:00 - 5:00 pm	Quick bite (BREAK)
5:00 - 6:00 pm	Complete pending school homework and assignments
6:00 - 7:00 pm	Take a break. Relax and play
7:00 - 7:30 pm	Have dinner
7:30 - 8:00 pm	Play
8:30 - 9:00 pm	Prepare for the next day. Wind up and get ready for bed

MATHS MASTERY STUDY SCHEDULER

Name:　　　　　　　　　　　　　　Grade:　　　　　　Date :

	MON	TUE	WED	THU	FRI	SAT	SUN
6:00 am	Wake Up	Wake Up	Wake Up	Wake Up	Wake Up		
6:00 - 7:00 am	Ready+Maths	Ready+Maths	Ready+Maths	Ready+Maths	Ready+Maths		
7:00 - 8:00 am	School	School	School	School	School		
8:00 - 9:00 am	School	School	School	School	School	Wake Up	Wake Up
9:00 - 10:00 am	School	School	School	School	School	Ready+Maths	Ready+Maths
10:00 - 11:00 am	School	School	School	School	School	Breakfast	Breakfast
11:00 - 12:00 pm	School	School	School	School	School	Study	Study
12:00 - 1:00 pm	School	School	School	School	School	BREAK	BREAK
1:00 - 2:00 pm	School	School	School	School	School	BREAK	BREAK
2:00 - 3:00 pm	School	School	School	School	School	BREAK	BREAK
3:00 - 4:00 pm	Back Home	Back Home	Back Home	Back Home	Back Home	Study	Study
4:00 - 5:00 pm	Eat + Maths	Eat + Maths	Eat + Maths	Eat + Maths	Eat + Maths	BREAK	BREAK
5:00 - 6:00 pm	School h/w	School h/w	School h/w	School h/w	School h/w	School h/w	School h/w
6:00 - 7:00 pm	BREAK	BREAK	BREAK	BREAK	BREAK	BREAK	BREAK
7:00 - 8:00 pm	Dinner	Dinner	Dinner	Dinner	Dinner	Dinner	Dinner
8:00 - 9:00 pm	BREAK	BREAK	BREAK	BREAK	BREAK	BREAK	BREAK
9:00 - 10:00 pm	Sleep	Sleep	Sleep	Sleep	Sleep	Sleep	Sleep

Step 3: On the second printout, outline how you envision your child's schedule based on the goals you aim to achieve. Don't worry if it is not perfect; you can use a pencil and make the necessary changes.

The success of this *Maths Mastery Study Scheduler* depends on how it is made and used. It doesn't have to be perfect. You can change things based on what's working and what's not. You can print more copies and refine it weekly or monthly. Remember, even though it's named a *Maths Mastery Study Scheduler*, you can apply this to anything your child wants to accomplish in life, not just excelling in maths. This step is crucial, so take your time and relish the process of supporting your child's success before moving to the next chapter.

Chapter 2.8

S8: Study Environment – Optimise

> *"The right study environment is not just a physical space; it's a mindset that encourages deep learning and growth." – Adam Grant*

Congratulations, dear parents! You've already covered 77.77% of the *S-9 Framework*. By following the first seven steps, you'll see great results in your child's progress. But the remaining 22.23% will make a massive difference in your child's maths skills and other areas of their life.

As parents, despite using study schedules and planners, you might still wonder why your child struggles to focus and concentrate. You may need clarification on what more you can do to support them.

This chapter will provide a "SCOOP" technique to guide your child towards the right environment. I encourage you to use this technique whenever your child studies, and I promise it will help your child excel. There are no magic solutions, just practical steps and support. Here's a technique to assist you:

Fig 2.8.1

S – Study Space (Dedicated)

It's common that despite parents providing space, guidance, and reminders, children may use it as expected only sometimes. This can be frustrating, but it's crucial to remember that children may need help understanding why this dedicated space is important. Open communication with your child is essential. Try to understand their concerns and feelings about the study area. By working together to tweak the study space, keeping it comfortable, and addressing your child's needs, you can encourage them to enjoy learning and fully appreciate the benefits of having a dedicated study area.

C – Calm Study Setting (Peaceful Environment)

Creating a calm study environment is crucial for effective learning. It's essential to have a peaceful and distraction-free place, especially during study time. When your child studies in such an environment, it helps them relax and focus better, leading to more effective studying without distractions.

Honest communication with your child is key. Discuss things that may disrupt their focus during study time and talk over how to deal with them. Together, you can make the study area quieter and more peaceful.

Consider setting specific times for maths sessions in your scheduler, like "Silent Hours". During these designated times, everyone in the house knows your child is studying, and they should try to minimise interruptions.

O – One Task Focus (No Multitasking)

In today's fast-paced world, where multitasking is a sign of efficiency, I understand how challenging it can be to keep your child from getting distracted and to help them focus on a single task. If you observe closely, you might face the same challenge. Just like it's hard to concentrate during prayer with distractions, your child may need help to focus on their studies. They might want to do anything besides study – drink water, use the restroom, talk about their school experiences, or suddenly feel aches and pains.

Here's a suggestion: Look at what distracts your child and what other tasks they're tempted to do while studying. Encourage them to delay those tasks and focus on maths first. In fact, I specifically advise parents to ensure their child drinks water, uses the restroom, and has a snack before starting to study. This way, they won't have any excuse to get distracted and can focus solely on their studies.

O – Organised Study Space (Clutter-free)

Ensuring your child's study space is organised is as crucial as having a well-arranged kitchen for cooking. Just as cooking becomes smoother with neatly arranged ingredients, the same concept applies to studying. The goal is to create a clutter-free space for focused learning.

Encourage your child to tidy up their study area before and after sessions. Use the *Maths Mastery Study Scheduler* to schedule regular clean-up sessions. Demonstrate and work with them initially, then encourage them to do it more independently with minimal assistance. This approach not only keeps the study area clutter-free but also fosters effective learning. Over time, it becomes a habit, leading to a naturally neat and organised study environment.

P – Prepared Supplies (Proper Stationery and Progress Trackers)

Ensure your child's study space stays organised by creating a checklist of their needs. While tidying up, ensure all items are in place and in good condition. Provide sharpened pencils, reliable erasers, working pens, staplers, and other essentials. Display the *"Maths Mastery Study Planner"* and *"Maths Mastery Study Scheduler"* for easy reference. Additionally, place a digital clock on the study table to facilitate time management. Having a digital clock on the study table prevents distractions caused by lifting devices to check the time. Encourage structured study sessions using a timer, like 25 minutes of focused study time followed by a 5-minute break, for smoother and more productive learning.

The following table concisely compares the key aspects of a proper study environment for each technique and how it differs from a less-than-ideal environment.

Optimising Your Child's Study Environment With
SCOOP TECHNIQUE

Technique	Aspects in a Proper Study Environment	Aspects in a Less-than-Ideal Environment
S - Study Space	A dedicated, organised study space	Lack of a dedicated study area-disorganised
C - Calm Environment	A peaceful and distraction-free study setting	Noisy and distracting study environment
O - One Task Focus	Focused on one task at a time	Frequent distractions and multitasking
O - Organized Study Space	Tidy and clutter-free study space	Cluttered and disorganized workspace
P - Prepared Supplies	Well-prepared stationery and accessible tools	Disorganised or missing supplies, ineffective progress tracking technique

Implementing these steps fosters a positive learning environment for your child's maths journey despite initial challenges. Over time, these practises become habitual, leading to significant improvements.

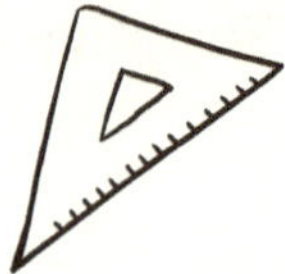

Chapter 2.9

S9: Study Guide – Create

> **"Consolidating formulas into a single reference can streamline your study process, making it easier to recall and apply them during exams." - Unknown**

In the final step of the *S-9 Framework*, we introduce a powerful tool – the *Study Guide*. Think of it as a treasure chest filled with maths formulas and example problems, neatly organised in one place. This guide is a secret weapon, especially for exam preparation.

You might wonder, *"Why do we need a study guide when we have textbooks and notebooks?"*

Research shows that a study guide helps children learn and remember maths better. It's like a recipe book in the kitchen, providing clear instructions and ingredient lists. Similarly, a study guide offers formulas and examples to solve maths problems. Creating a study guide helps your child recall and refresh their understanding before exams, much like using tried-and-true recipes when cooking. It's a valuable resource that simplifies maths learning.

HOW TO CREATE A STUDY GUIDE:

Creating a study guide won't take too much of your time. It's a straight forward task. Follow these easy steps, and you'll quickly have a helpful guide.

Your guide doesn't need to be perfect from the start. Think of it as a journey, similar to your child's maths learning journey. It's a work in progress that evolves over time. Here's a step-by-step plan you can follow:

1. *Utilise the Maths Mastery Study Planner:* Remember the Study Planner from Step 4? It's a helpful tool. Use it to list all the maths topics and their formulas. This way, when your child faces a tricky problem, they can refer to the guide and understand how to solve it.

2. *Organise Neatly:* Keep the information tidy in a notebook or folder. Use clear headings and labels for each topic, making it easy for your child to find what they need quickly.

3. *Include Example Problems:* Add example problems for each formula or concept—these act as practical guides, showing your child how to apply the formula in real situations.

4. *Keep It Updated:* Update the study guide as your child learns new maths concepts. It should always reflect their current understanding of maths.

Making a study guide is like giving your child a helpful present. It helps them understand and remember maths better and makes tough problems easier. It's a simple but strong tool for success. Don't worry if it's not perfect at first. Your child can keep adding more formulas and examples later on.

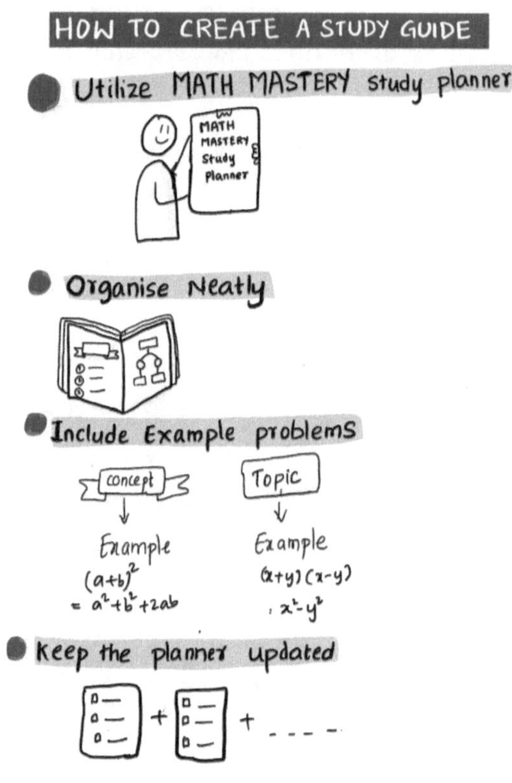

Fig 2.9.1

SECTION 3

FEARS AND STRESS

Chapter 3.1

Understanding Fears

If you've been following along, you might be starting to understand why your child has yet to achieve good maths scores. Initially, you might have thought it was because they weren't interested or couldn't concentrate. But now, you might realise that they could be facing external and internal challenges, as discussed in Chapter 2.5.

While Section 2 of the book focused on external challenges, this chapter delves into internal challenges, i.e., the fears and worries that your child or you as parents might face. The next chapter will explore overcoming these fears together.

Think of it like this: Imagine your child loves playing soccer, but they're always nervous about making mistakes or not playing well. These internal fears affect their performance and stop them from fully enjoying the game. Similarly, in maths, some children have worries and anxieties that make them nervous, affecting their ability to do their best.

FEARS OF CHILDREN

1. **Fear of Failure:**

   Children might fear making mistakes or getting low grades on maths tests. It's like in soccer, where if they fear failing, they might not try their best. This holds them back from getting perfect scores.

2. **Fear of Mathematics Itself:**

   Some children simply don't like maths, similar to not enjoying a favourite food. When children have negative feelings towards maths, it's hard for them to do well and reach their full potential.

3. **Fear of Performance:**

   If they make mistakes, kids might worry that others will think they're not good at maths. This fear can make it hard for them to concentrate and do well, especially during tests. They're afraid of making mistakes in front of others, which stops them from getting the scores they can actually get.

4. **Fear of the Unknown:**

   Imagine your child was given a puzzle but had no idea how to solve it. They would feel uncertain and maybe even anxious. The same thing happens with maths problems. When kids don't know how to solve them, it can trigger anxiety and fear, making it hard for them to reach their potential.

5. **Maths Trauma:**

   Sometimes, kids have had bad experiences with maths. They might have been embarrassed or punished for making mistakes. These experiences can create a deep fear or dislike of maths. Just like having a bad experience with one dog can make you scared of all dogs, past negative experiences can affect a child's progress in maths.

Before moving to the next chapter, which will help you understand and conquer these fears, let's know that there are a few fears that parents might unknowingly have. When a child senses these fears in their parents, it can also become the child's fear.

FEARS OF PARENTS

1. **Fear of Falling Behind:**

   Parents worry that if their children don't do well in maths, they might fall behind their peers or miss critical educational opportunities. They fear their child won't be able to fill the gap and keep up with the curriculum or future academic challenges.

2. **Fear of Inability to Help:**

Parents who've struggled with maths themselves, fear they won't be able to support or assist their children. They worry about being unable to answer their children's questions or provide the guidance needed to overcome maths challenges.

3. **Fear of Negative Judgement:**

Parents may fear that their children's poor performance in maths will reflect poorly on them as parents. They worry about being judged by others and feel pressured to ensure their children succeed in all subjects, including maths.

4. **Fear of Losing Confidence:**

Parents want their children to have confidence in their abilities. If their children constantly struggle with maths, parents may fear it will erode their children's self-confidence and belief in their academic abilities.

Now that you know the broader categories of fear, the next chapter will guide you on a journey to help you and your child overcome these fears and anxieties and become more confident in maths. By doing so, you can help your child unlock their true potential, become good at maths, and experience the joy of academic success.

Chapter 3.2

Tips for Overcoming Fears

Overcoming fears, especially the fear of maths, can be challenging for both parents and children. However, with determination and the right approach, it's possible. This chapter offers simple tips and strategies for parents and children to address their fears and build confidence in maths.

We'll explore a helpful method for parents called PROGRESS, akin to a roadmap to support both you and your child to overcome your fears. Let's delve into each part of the **PROGRESS** technique and discover how it can help you assist your child better.

P – Pinpoint the Source of Fear:

Take the time to understand what makes your child afraid of maths. Think about when it started, what makes them nervous, and what exactly they're scared of. This will help you make a plan to help them feel better.

For example, have a chat with your child about how they feel about maths. Figure out when they started feeling scared and what makes them worry. By knowing what's bothering them, you can find ways to help. This makes them feel more in control and less anxious about maths.

R – Reflect on Individual Progress:

Think about how your child is progressing in their learning journey and how they've developed their individual skills. Appreciate and motivate your child's efforts. Instead of comparing them to others, focus on their progress and growth.

For example, if your child had difficulty with addition at the beginning of the year but can now solve problems confidently, that's something to celebrate! Remember, every child learns differently and at their own pace.

O – Organise Time with Breaks:

Managing time is crucial to avoid last-minute tasks piling up. Assist your child in wisely managing their time by incorporating breaks for relaxation and renewal.

For example, create a weekly plan with dedicated time slots for assisting your child with maths. Prioritise this, ensuring that your child focuses solely on their maths work during these sessions. Let your child take a 5-minute break for every 25 minutes of studying. Encourage them to engage in an activity they enjoy, such as playing outside, listening to music, or reading a book. These breaks help prevent mental fatigue and promote a more relaxed approach to maths.

G – Gradually Introduce Challenges:

Help your child develop their maths skills by gradually introducing new concepts and challenges. By gradually exposing your child to increasingly complex concepts, you can build their confidence and competence in maths.

For example, start with basic multiplication problems, such as 2 * 3, and then gradually progress to more advanced topics like multiplication of fractions, such as 1/2 * 3/4.

R – Realistic Goal Setting:

Encourage your child to set goals that are achievable and inspire them to succeed. By setting attainable goals and tracking their progress, you can observe how your child is advancing and boost their confidence along the way.

For example, if your child struggles with multiplication, a realistic goal could be to memorise the tables up to 5 by the end of the month. Break down the maths curriculum into smaller, manageable objectives, such as mastering one table at a time.

E – Embrace Growth Mindset:

Encourage your child to adopt a growth mindset, viewing challenges as opportunities for learning and improvement. Shift the focus from grades to effort and progress. Teach your child that mistakes and struggles are natural parts of the learning process and opportunities for growth. By fostering persistence and resilience, you can help them overcome challenges and build confidence in their maths abilities.

For example, instead of solely focusing on your child's low marks, take a moment to reflect on their progress. Consider where your child started and acknowledge the skills they have developed by dedicating time and effort to understanding the material and improving their skills.

S – Supportive Environment:

Create a supportive and nurturing atmosphere at home to encourage your child's learning and growth. Foster positivity and encouragement and celebrate their efforts and achievements in all subjects, including maths. Offer specific praise for their problem-solving skills and resilience, motivating them to excel in maths tasks. Additionally, maintain an open and understanding environment where your child feels comfortable seeking help or expressing frustrations.

For instance, when your child faces maths difficulties, listen attentively and provide reassurance. Offer guidance without criticism, emphasising that mistakes are part of learning. Celebrate their progress, such as completing a challenging assignment, with words of encouragement or a small reward. This positive reinforcement boosts confidence and reduces maths-related anxiety.

S – Seek Professional Assistance:

Feel free to seek help from teachers or professionals when needed. But while seeking assistance, ensure that the focus is on making your child independent in their learning through this collaboration. Encourage them to become skilled in analysing new concepts and studying independently, empowering them to become confident learners.

Fig 3.2.1

Parent: "Hey, my love. I've noticed you've been feeling a bit stressed about maths lately. Can you help me understand why it's been tough for you?"

Child: "Ugh, I just really don't like maths. It's hard, and I always feel like I will make mistakes."

Parent: "I hear you. Let's talk more about it. Why do you think maths is hard for you, and why does it feel like you might again make mistakes?"

Child: "I don't know. It's just scary with all those numbers and problems. It feels like too much."

Parent: "I can imagine it feels overwhelming. Can you share more? Why does it feel so scary? And why is doing well in maths important to you?"

Child: "I want to make you proud and do well in school."

Parent: "Thank you for opening up. Let's keep going. Why is making me proud and doing well in school important to you? And why do you worry that you might not already be doing this?"

Child: "When I couldn't solve a problem in class, everyone laughed at me. It made me feel dumb."

Parent: "Oh, sweetheart, I'm so sorry you went through that. I understand, at that moment, you felt dumb."

Child: "Yes. And I don't want people to laugh at me. It's embarrassing."

Parent: "Is it ok if we talk more? Tell me, if you don't want people to laugh at you, what do you want?"

Child: "I don't want to feel dumb. I just want to be good at something. But I don't know how."

Parent: "Do you want to overcome this fear and feel confident? In Maths?"

Child: "Yes. I want to stop feeling dumb. I want to prove that I can do it."

Parent: "That's good. Tell me why you believe you can do well in maths."

Child: "Sometimes, when I get a maths problem right, it feels perfect."

Parent: "So, do you believe you can have more of them?"

Child: "Yes. I know I can do it if I try a little more."

Parent: "That's the spirit! You're incredible, and I'm here with you every step. Together, we'll conquer that fear, and maths will become something you truly enjoy. I believe in you more than you can imagine."

The chapter emphasises the importance of open and empathetic conversations with your child about their maths fears. Using the "why" strategy and asking thoughtful questions helps uncover the root cause of their anxiety. Assure your child that mistakes are normal in learning and that their worth isn't tied to maths skills.

Chapter 3.3

Stress Reduction Strategies

Mathematics often triggers anxiety and stress, impacting both students and their parents. Parental stress in maths education can arise from various sources such as unresolved maths issues, societal pressure, and the focus on test results. These factors overshadow the joy of learning maths.

To alleviate stress, parents can implement various techniques. This chapter will guide you with a few stress reduction strategies to foster a positive learning environment. By integrating these proven strategies, parents can reduce stress, instil a positive mindset, and nurture a love for maths.

While the PROGRESS technique helps overcome fears, the PEACE technique offers additional stress-reducing methods. These holistic approaches promote calmness and confidence, enhancing a child's emotional well-being and academic success. Let's delve into each aspect of the PEACE technique to support children in mastering maths and beyond.

P: Positive Affirmations

You can help your children by encouraging them to shift their focus from fears to positive thoughts and affirmations. Encourage them to repeat positive statements to themselves. If they struggle, you can repeat these affirmations for them.

For example, motivate your child to replace negative thoughts with positive affirmations like "*I can do this*" or "*Maths is fun and exciting.*"

More about Positive Affirmations and their benefits will be shared in the upcoming chapters.

E: Easing Stress with Breathing and Relaxation

Teach your child simple relaxation techniques for when they feel stressed about maths. Encourage slow, deep breathing and counting to 10, as these methods calm the body and reduce anxiety.

For example, guide your child through breathing exercises: inhale slowly through the nose, then exhale through the mouth. If you both feel overwhelmed by maths homework, take a moment together to sit quietly. Close your eyes and take a deep breath through your nose, holding it briefly before exhaling slowly through the mouth. Repeat this process a few times to relax before resuming your work together.

A: Attuning to Mindfulness and Meditation

Introduce mindfulness techniques or short meditation exercises for both you and your child to practise together, aiding in calming the mind and reducing stress.

For example, consider downloading a mindfulness app or finding guided meditation videos online that both you and your child can use. Set aside a few minutes each day to sit quietly, focusing on your breath, or following a guided meditation. This joint practise allows both, the parent and child, to let go of stressful thoughts and be fully present in the moment.

C: Cultivating Visualisation Techniques

Introduce simple visualisation exercises for both you and your child to practise, which aid in reducing anxiety and improving maths performance.

For instance, guide your child to imagine themselves confidently solving a maths problem or achieving a good grade. Encourage them to visualise the steps they would take and the positive outcome they desire.

More about visualisation techniques and their benefits will be shared in the upcoming chapters.

E: Engaging in Physical Activity

Even with busy schedules, finding light and easy physical activities can greatly benefit both parents and children in reducing stress.

For instance, consider activities like taking short walks together around the neighbourhood, doing some gentle stretching exercises at home, or having a quick dance session to your child's favourite music. These simple activities can fit into tight schedules and still provide the stress-relieving benefits of physical activity.

Fig 3.3.1

Overcoming fears takes time and effort, but with patience and persistence, it's possible. By following these strategies, parents can effectively support their children in overcoming maths fears.

SECTION 4

MASTERING EXAMS

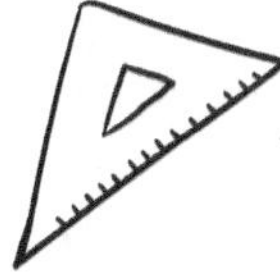

Chapter 4.1

Preparation Mastery

Now that we've discussed overcoming fears and worries around maths, and have learned some practical stress reduction strategies, let's explore how to help your child prepare for their exams. Taking an exam is like creating a piece of art—a skill children cannot develop solely in the exam room. If not done correctly, it could lead to a disappointing outcome. Hence, training children to prepare for exams and approach the writing process is crucial. Training doesn't mean pressuring them to aim only for full marks; it involves helping your child strategize. This not only aids in tackling exams but also develops problem-solving skills applicable to board games, facing challenges, learning, and more.

Many parents and students, unaware of the right approach, worry and invest significant efforts in exam preparation. Unfortunately, most of the time when their children's results are out, they don't reflect the effort put in, which leads to disappointment. You will find straightforward, simple techniques in this chapter that anyone can follow. If you can help your child start practising one-on-one techniques, you will begin to see improvement in their scores. However, it's essential to emphasise that it's all about practise; the more they practise the technique, the better their performance will become.

A: Always Know the Exam Format

Before the exam, ensure your child understands the test format, including the number and types of questions and the allotted time. This information helps them plan how to allocate their time effectively during the exam.

For example, ask them how many problem-solving and multiple-choice questions they expect in the test and how much time they'll have for each.

B: Brush Up the Course Material:

Ensure your child has a firm grasp of the course material, focusing on formulae, concepts, and problem-solving strategies. Prioritise areas where they feel less confident. Class notes and the *Study Guide* created in *Step 9* can help summarise the key concepts and formulae covered in class. Ensure they review the notes regularly and use them to reinforce their understanding of the material.

For example, if they are studying geometry, ask them to explain the Pythagorean theorem or recall key formulas for finding area and perimeter.

C: Conduct Mock Tests:

Encourage your child to solve sample papers under exam conditions – with a timer and without access to external resources. This practise helps identify areas of improvement and refine study habits. (Step 7 of the framework covers more on this). Remember, practising here means active writing and solving, not just going through the material. Step 6 explains this in detail.

D: Discover Weaknesses and Tackle Them:

Review your child's performance in sample papers. Guide them to focus on the challenging areas during study sessions, ensuring they understand them thoroughly.

For example, they should spend extra time on geometry concepts during study sessions if they struggle with geometry questions. Ask them to explain their thought process when solving such problems.

E: Efficient Time Management:

While they are answering the mock test, you can keep an eye on the clock and ensure they have a good sense of how long each question type takes. Then, guide your child with a rough estimate of time allocation for each exam section. Practise will help them follow the timeline during an exam.

For instance, suggest they spend 30 minutes on problem-solving and 20 minutes on multiple-choice questions. During practise sessions, observe how well they adhere to this timeline.

F: Focus on Instructions:

Train your child to read each question twice, underlining important parts and following any special instructions. Ensure they understand the question before answering it and encourage them not to hesitate to seek clarification from the teacher.

G: Give Every Question Its Time:

Emphasise spending a good amount of time on each question. Guide them in showing their work in detail and explain their thought process as they solve each problem. This helps them check their work and demonstrates their understanding of the material to the examiners. They should be made to practise double-checking their work before moving on to the next question, which ensures accuracy and minimises errors.

H: Handle the Easy Questions First:

Guide your child to start with the questions they know well, i.e., by answering the questions that appear easier or more familiar. This will help build confidence and ensure that relatively simple marks are secured early on.

For example, if the test includes a multiple-choice section, begin by answering those questions. This allows for quick progress and a positive momentum to carry forward.

I: If a Question's Tough, Take It Step by Step:

Guide your child to stay calm if they find a tricky question. Educate them break it down into smaller parts and then tackle each part one by one.

For example, let the child break down the question, analyse each component, and use any available formulas, concepts, or problem-solving techniques to approach it step by step.

J: Just Before You Finish, Check Again:

Remind your child to save some time at the end for reviewing the answers. This step helps catch mistakes and ensures a thorough understanding of the questions. Let them not just glance and believe whatever they've written is correct. Let them take the time to go through each answer, ensuring accuracy and coherence. Cross-verify calculations and confirm they have answered all the questions.

For example, your child should reread each question and verify that the answer provided addresses the specific requirements. Your child should also review calculations for errors and ensure that all steps are clear and logical.

Fig 4.1.1

By following these steps, you can assist your child in understanding the exam format, preparing effectively, and improving their scores. Parents and students often worry about insufficient time during exams to attempt all the questions. However, by practising effective time management techniques, your child can finish the paper on time and have ample opportunity to review and re-check their work. Trust in this process, as I've personally used these techniques and witnessed students excel in their studies using them. With consistent practise, you'll see the positive results reflected in your child's improved scores.

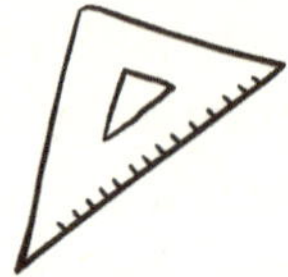

Chapter 4.2

Exam Day Mastery

Throughout my journey as a student and now as an academic strategist, I've witnessed first-hand how careful preparation and a calm mindset on exam day can make all the difference. In my role, I've assisted students and parents in navigating the challenges of maths exams, emphasising the significance of simple yet often overlooked strategies. Confidence is key, and this chapter is dedicated to sharing practical tips that have proven effective in reducing stress and helping students achieve perfect scores, sometimes even a perfect 100. Many parents have shared their personal experiences and their children's achievements after implementing these strategies. Let's walk through it together and make maths exams less intimidating for students and parents alike.

A – Arrive Early:

Arriving early at the exam venue and being mentally prepared helps your child stay calm and do well. It allows them to enter the exam hall with a focused mindset, ready to perform their best. Arriving early also allows them to settle in and review any last-minute notes or concepts.

For example, if an exam starts at 9 am, arriving at least 30 minutes before the scheduled time allows students to find their seats, organise their materials, and prepare themselves mentally.

B – Breathe and Relax:

Encourage your child to calm their mind using deep breathing techniques before the exam.

For example, they can take deep breaths through the nose, hold for a few seconds, and exhale slowly.

C – Cope With Stress:

Stress can affect performance during the exam. Implementing strategies like *efficient time management, focusing on the instructions, giving every question its time, handling the easy questions first, if a question is tough, taking it step by step, and checking the paper again before submitting* will help your child stay calm and focused, maximising their potential. These are all discussed in detail in Chapter 4.1.

D – Drink Water:

Keeping hydrated is essential for optimal brain function. Encourage your child to keep a small water bottle handy and take sips when needed.

For example, they can drink water after every 30 minutes or after answering a few questions.

E – Encourage Positive Self-Talk:

Guide your child to use positive self-talk to reinforce confidence and belief in their preparation.

For example, they can close their eyes, take a deep breath, and remind themselves, "I have prepared for this question, and I can do it."

F – Focus and Try Again:

If your child encounters a question they're unsure about, encourage them not to panic. Instead, they can close their eyes, try to recall the related information, and attempt the question based on what they remember. Even partial answers can earn valuable marks.

For example, they can visualise the concepts and try to solve as many problems as possible. Retaining trust in their preparation, reinforcing positive self-talk, and making the best attempt possible will alleviate stress and allow them to perform at their best.

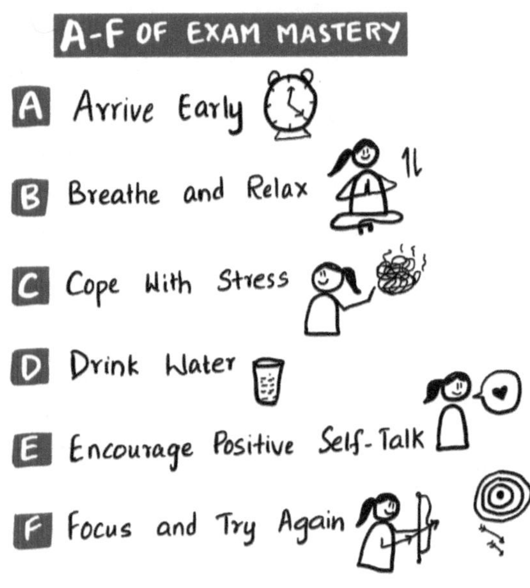

Fig 4.2.1

By incorporating these strategies, your child can stay calm, focused, and confident during exams, increasing their chances of success not only in maths but any school or competitive exam they face.

SECTION 5

MINDFULNESS AND HAPPINESS

Chapter 5.1

Affirmations

Affirmations can be a powerful tool for building confidence and reducing stress. Affirmations are like magic words that can make a big difference for your child. Whether you are good at maths or not, you as a parent, can help your child feel confident and do well in it. When parents affirm their child's ability to score a 100/100 in maths, they send a powerful message of belief and encouragement. When you tell your child that they can get a perfect score in maths, it shows you believe in them. That makes them feel good about themselves and helps them do better in school. It's like giving them a boost of confidence to tackle any problem that comes their way. When you show interest and excitement about your child's maths journey, they see it as fun and not scary. That makes them want to learn more and do their best. So, when your child faces challenging maths problems, your words of encouragement using positive affirmations can keep them going. They'll keep trying until they find the answer. Overall, by giving positive affirmations regularly, you're helping your child feel good about themselves and do well in school. It's like giving them a secret weapon to tackle any maths problem and succeed.

Here are some sample positive affirmations that your children can themselves say and make them a part of their daily routine.

Positive Affirmations for Your Child for Maths Practise:

- I am getting better at maths every day.

- Maths becomes easier for me with each practise session.

- I understand and grasp maths concepts effortlessly.

- The more I engage with maths, the more it makes sense to me.

- I enjoy learning and exploring maths; it brings me joy.

- Maths is like a puzzle that excites me to unravel and solve.

- Complex maths concepts are within my reach and understanding.

- Maths helps me think critically and solve problems effectively.

- I am open to learning new maths techniques and strategies.

- I trust in my ability to use maths in real-life situations.

- Maths is like a language that I am becoming fluent in.

- I am surrounded by a supportive community that encourages my love for maths.

- Maths helps me understand and interpret the world around me.

- I have the potential to achieve remarkable success in maths.

Positive Re-Affirmations for Your Child Before Maths Tests:

- I am fully prepared for my upcoming maths test.

- I am confident that I will excel in my maths test.

- I can tackle any maths challenge that comes my way.

- I am determined to study hard and do my best on my maths exam.

- I am a dedicated and motivated maths student.

- I embrace challenges in maths as opportunities for growth.

- My maths skills will pave the way for my future career success.

- I have the necessary skills and knowledge to excel in maths tests.

- No matter the size of my progress, I am proud of my achievements in maths.

- I am resilient and can overcome any maths difficulties I encounter.

You may wonder how to ensure they become a regular part of your child's routine. One effective way is to encourage your child to repeat these affirmations daily. Repetition is powerful—it helps reinforce positive beliefs and attitudes, making them more deeply ingrained in your child's mindset.

Consider creating a particular time each day for your child to affirm these. It could be in the morning before their maths practise or in the evening before bed. Encourage them to say the affirmations out loud or silently to themselves, whichever feels most comfortable.

To make the affirmations even more impactful, I suggest that you or your child write them down in a journal or on sticky notes that they can place around their room. This way, they'll be reminded of these positive messages throughout the day, reinforcing their confidence and belief in themselves.

Now that you have these powerful affirmations to boost your child's confidence, let's discuss some re-affirmations. Re-affirmations are positive words or phrases that you can say to your child again and again to help them feel good about maths. These words of encouragement can reinforce their belief in themselves and their abilities, making learning maths more enjoyable and less daunting.

Positive Affirmations for Parents for Maths Practise:

- You are so smart, and I know you can do great maths. I believe in you.

- I see how hard you work in maths, and it pays off. You're doing amazing.

- I'm here for you every step of the way as you learn maths. I know you can keep getting better and better.

- I do not doubt that you are good at maths.

- Wow, you're getting better and better at maths every day. You have all the skills and determination to do incredible things.

- You're a natural at maths, and I believe you can achieve anything you set your mind to.

- Keep practising maths, and I'm so proud of how far you've come. You're doing a fantastic job.

Positive Re-Affirmations for Parents Before Maths Tests:

- I'm proud of your progress in maths, and I know you can reach your goal in your upcoming test.

- Your hard work and dedication in maths will pay off in your exam. You've got this!

- I have complete faith in your abilities and know that you can ace your maths test.

- You've studied diligently for your maths exam, and I'm confident that you will excel.

- Take a deep breath, trust in yourself, and remember that you are fully prepared for your maths test.

- Believe in your abilities and approach your maths test with confidence. You are capable of great things.

- No matter what the outcome of your maths test, I am proud of your efforts and growth in this subject.

- Use your knowledge and skills to tackle each maths problem confidently. You can conquer this test!

As a parent, you can also read these affirmations aloud with your child. This shows your support and sets a positive example of self-affirmation and self-belief. Together, using these positive affirmations, you and your child can create a daily routine that fosters a strong sense of confidence and resilience, setting them up for success in maths and all the areas of their life.

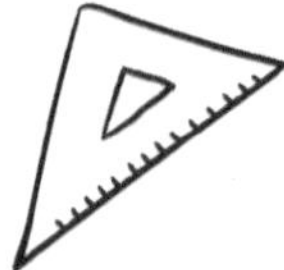

Chapter 5.2

Visualisations

Visualisation is a powerful tool that can assist children in achieving their goals and succeeding in various aspects of life, including academics. Even for parents without formal education, understanding and applying visualisation techniques can greatly benefit their children's academic journey. Let's explore how visualisation works and how parents can utilise it effectively.

When you visualise your child scoring a perfect 100/100 in maths, you are not just daydreaming – you are creating a positive mental image that can significantly impact your child's focus, motivation, and, ultimately, success in mathematics. This positive mental imagery will help your child develop what psychologists call a "growth mindset", where challenges are opportunities for growth rather than obstacles to overcome. It instils resilience and perseverance, crucial qualities for academic achievement.

Moreover, visualising your child excelling in maths creates a supportive environment around them, fostering a positive attitude towards the subject. A positive attitude towards maths is a strong predictor of academic success. By nurturing this mindset through visualisation, you can set your child up for success in maths and other educational endeavours.

Furthermore, visualisation can help alleviate the fear and anxiety often associated with maths. When children visualise themselves solving maths problems successfully and achieving their goals, it boosts their confidence and reduces stress. This sense of confidence and calmness enhances their performance during exams and assessments.

In essence, visualisation is a powerful tool for parents to empower their children in maths and beyond. By creating mental images of success and nurturing a positive mindset, parents can give their children the skills, attitude, and belief they need to excel in mathematics and other areas of life.

Let's explore a simple visualisation exercise that parents can practise to help their child achieve a perfect score in maths:

> *Close your eyes and imagine your child sitting at their desk, fully focused and feeling sure of themselves as they work on their maths problems. With each correct answer, they show excitement and interest, powered by the happiness of doing well. Picture them finishing the test quickly and rechecking their answers with a smile before handing it in.*
>
> *Now, think about the day the results are announced. Your child has done well on the test, getting a perfect score of 100/100! You can feel the pride and happiness on their face as you congratulate them on their success. You also feel happy knowing their effort and determination have paid off.*

Now, let's consider a visualisation exercise that you can use for your child to help them excel in maths:

> *Close your eyes and imagine yourself studying hard for your maths test. Feel the confidence building inside you as you understand each concept and solve every problem. Sitting down to take the test makes you feel calm and focused because you know you've prepared well.*
>
> *You answer each question quickly and accurately, satisfied with every correct response. You take your time, rechecking your work to ensure it's accurate. As the test ends, you feel excited and sure you did well.*
>
> *When the results are out, you smile with pride when you see the perfect score, 100/100! Your effort and determination have paid off, and you share the good news with your family, enjoying their praise and support.*

Visualisation is not just wishful thinking; it's a powerful technique, backed by science, which can propel children toward academic success. So go ahead, visualise the optimistic outcome, and watch your child's dreams turn into reality through the magic of visualisation.

Chapter 5.3

Happy Hormones and Maths

When we think about maths, we often imagine tough numbers and strict rules. It is a tricky subject that makes children worry. But what if we change this idea? What if maths could make your child happy and excited?

In this chapter, we'll talk about how solving maths problems can make your child feel comfortable. Special chemicals in our brains called *"happy hormones"* are responsible for making us feel good. There are four main types of these happy hormones:

Each of these hormones makes us feel differently, and we'll explain how maths can help release them, which can create a happier and more enjoyable learning experience for your child. So, let us explore how maths can bring happiness to your child!

Serotonin:

Just like when your child eats their favourite cake or wins a game they love, their brain releases serotonin, making them feel good. In the same way, when they solve a maths problem, their brain releases serotonin, making them feel happy.

Tips for Parents: Encourage and celebrate your child's maths successes, big or small. That boosts serotonin and keeps them comfortable while learning.

Endorphins

When your child conquers a challenge like reaching the top of a high slide, their body releases endorphins, making them feel relaxed. Similarly, solving a challenging maths problem can release endorphins, helping them feel calm and content.

Tips for Parents: Turn maths into an enjoyable activity, like a game or a fun challenge. This triggers the release of endorphins, making maths feel relaxing and enjoyable for your child.

Dopamine:

When your child wins a game, they feel excited, which triggers the release of dopamine in their brain, keeping them motivated. Solving a maths problem can also set off dopamine release, boosting motivation and happiness.

Tips for Parents: Make maths problems feel like a fun game or challenge. This stimulates dopamine release, keeping your child engaged and motivated to learn.

Oxytocin:

When your child plays with friends, their brain releases oxytocin, fostering closeness and connection. Working on maths problems with a friend can also trigger oxytocin release, helping them feel connected and happy.

Tips for Parents: Encourage collaborative maths activities with friends. This promotes oxytocin release, strengthens friendships, and makes maths more enjoyable.

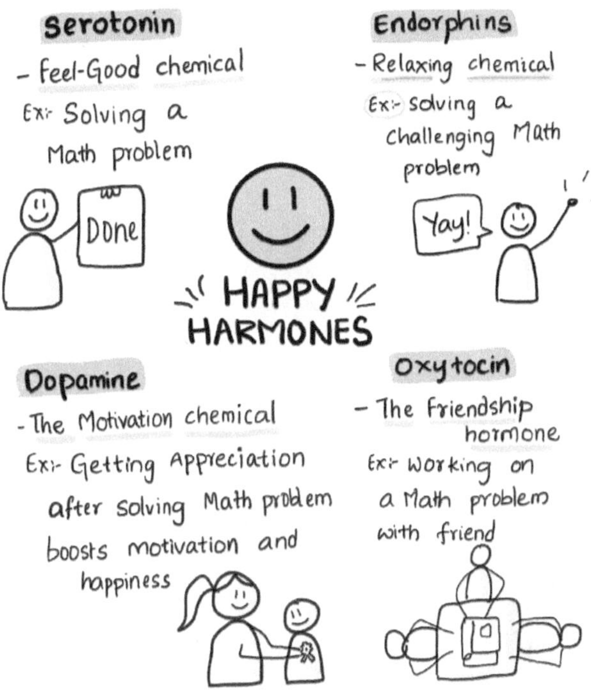

Fig 5.3.1

As you can see, maths is more than just numbers. It can make your child feel happy, relaxed, motivated, and even help them get along with others. Understanding this can help us see maths in a new way. By harnessing the power of happy hormones like serotonin, endorphins, dopamine, and oxytocin, parents can create a positive and supportive environment where maths becomes a source of joy, motivation, and friendship for their children. Let's continue to embrace the happiness that maths can bring and cultivate a lifelong love for learning.

Conclusion

Maths isn't just about achieving perfect scores. It's about cultivating a love for learning and aiding your child's growth. It's about encouraging them to embrace challenges, learn from their mistakes, and celebrate every step of their progress. However, despite these broader goals, as parents, you all still desire your children to perform well in maths exams and aim for perfection. The reasons for this aspiration may vary from one parent to another.

While many of you may already be familiar with the concepts discussed in this book, it's important to recognise that mere knowledge isn't enough. Action is what truly matters. In today's digital age, despite knowing what you want for your child, it's easy to get distracted and lose sight of your goals. Helping your child succeed in maths, or any endeavour, for that matter, is akin to navigating a winding road. It requires unwavering focus and determination. By initiating awareness and determination from the beginning, you can help your child navigate their journey, overcoming any challenges they may face.

Whether you choose to guide your child independently or seek assistance from professionals, the key lies in following the *S-9 Framework* and implementing the tips provided in this book. Rest assured that with consistent effort, your child will gradually improve their performance in maths exams. Trust in the process, believe in your child's abilities, and celebrate their journey.

15 Rules for Maths Mastery

1. **Start Early:** Begin teaching maths concepts at a young age and maintain a positive attitude towards maths. *[Chapter 1.1]*

2. **Set Goals and Believe in Your Child:** Establish clear objectives and have confidence in your child's ability to learn maths. *[Chapter 2.1]*

3. **Identify Strengths and Weaknesses:** Recognise areas where your child excels and where they need improvement in maths. *[Chapter 2.2]*

4. **Build a Solid Foundation:** Focus on laying a solid groundwork in fundamental maths concepts. *[Chapter 2.3]*

5. **Make and Follow a Plan:** Create a structured plan for your child's maths education and monitor their progress regularly. *[Chapter 2.4]*

6. **Focus and Review Mistakes:** Identify the challenges your child is facing and the mistakes they are making. *[Chapter 2.5]*

7. **Practise Similar Problems:** Encourage consistent and deliberate practise of maths skills. *[Chapter 2.6]*

8. **Allocate Daily Time for Maths:** Dedicate a specific time each day for maths practise and study. *[Chapter 2.7]*

9. **Create a Positive Study Environment:** Cultivate a supportive and encouraging atmosphere for learning maths. Acknowledge and celebrate your child's accomplishments, no matter how small. *[Chapter 2.8]*

10. **Keep a Study Guide Handy:** Maintain a reference guide for quick review before exams or assessments. *[Chapter 2.9]*

11. **Address Fears and Stress:** Understand and help your child overcome any fears or anxieties related to maths. *[Section 3]*

12. **Strategize and Prepare for Exams:** Develop effective study strategies and preparation techniques for maths exams. *[Chapter 4.1]*

13. **Follow Exam Guidelines:** Ensure your child understands and adheres to the rules during maths exams. *[Chapter 4.2]*

14. **Stay Positive:** Maintain a positive outlook on maths learning and outcomes. *[Chapter 5.1]*

15. **Visualise Success:** Encourage your child to visualise achieving their maths goals and attracting positive results. *[Chapter 5.2]*

Before we conclude, I want to express my gratitude to you for placing your trust in me and this book. If this book has inspired you to make positive changes, then it has achieved its purpose. My hope is that through this book, you not only learn how to support your child in maths but also take actionable steps to enhance their mathematical skills.

Together, let's continue advancing forward.

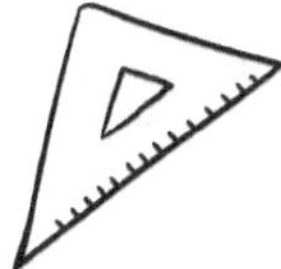

Acknowledgements

It takes a village to raise a child, and it took an army of givers to complete this book. In writing this book, I have been blessed with the love, assistance, and guidance of many individuals who have profoundly touched my life, taught me, and worked with me over the years. I wish to express my heartfelt thanks to every one of you.

First and foremost, I owe an immense debt of gratitude to my husband, Akshay Agarwal. He read and re-read the chapters with patience and offered valuable feedback. Despite the demands of our busy lives and the responsibilities of raising our two wonderful daughters, Aashka and Anaisha, he has stood by me every step of the way, providing invaluable insights and support. I am blessed for all the love and happiness they bring into my life, making me better every day.

I extend this book as a token of gratitude to my grandparents, parents, in-laws, and my entire family, whose unwavering love and backing have made this journey possible. A special mention goes to my official guardian, Kamini Gupta, and my mentor, Pratibha Sharma, for their guidance and mentorship. Thank you all from the bottom of my heart.

I am immensely grateful to all my friends, colleagues, and my team, who supported me behind the scenes with feedback, suggestions, and encouragement throughout the journey. Your belief in me and your willingness to lend a hand has not gone unnoticed. As there are too many names to mention, I will limit to the most specific acknowledgements for those who read and commented on the portion of this manuscript.

I extend my deepest thanks to my dearest friend, Aanjali Wadhwani, who has helped organise this book from its inception to finish, going beyond the call of her duty. My friend Debaleena Das, for her unwavering guidance and encouragement at every turn, pushed me to complete the book. I am also indebted to my dear friend, Nikhil Dabhade, whose insights and willingness to challenge me to think deeper and write better have been instrumental in brainstorming the framing of the book's content. I thank Lavanya Reddy for her striking illustrations that bring the book to life.

My gratitude extends to all the students and parents who approached me with numerous questions and discussed the challenges they encountered during exams and on a day-to-day basis. All of this enabled me to delve deeper into the current research.

Lastly, I thank all those who will read this book and pass it on to others. I sincerely hope the words within these pages will inspire and empower you to help your child.

With deepest gratitude,

Amrita Agarwal